DATE DUE

DEMCO 38-296

Organizing
for
Political
Victory

Organizing for Political Victory

Loren B. Belker

Nelson-Hall nh **Chicago**

LIBRARY OF CONGRESS CATALOGING IN PUBLICATION DATA

Belker, Loren B.
  Organizing for political victory.

  Includes index.
  1. Campaign management. I. Title.
  JF2112. C3B44   324.7'8   82-7855
  ISBN 0-88229-727-9   AACR2

Copyright © 1982 by Loren B. Belker

Manufactured in the United States of America

10 9 8 7 6 5 4 3 2 1

The paper in this book is pH neutral (acid-free).

This book is dedicated to my parents and to the person who makes the political system work — the campaign volunteer.

Contents

Foreword

RUNNING FOR POLITICAL OFFICE, like much of our society, has become much more complex than it was even twenty years ago. A candidate who enters a political campaign too casually will soon find that it is expensive, and both mentally and physically exhausting.

A political campaign is the opportunity for the voters to find out what kind of candidate is asking for their support. That candidate needs to put his or her best foot forward, and to clearly articulate positions on the issues involved. A candidate who becomes too mired down in the details of the campaign misses the opportunity to meet the voters and explain his or her position on the issues. But yet a candidate must be aware of what goes into a thorough and successful campaign.

While some campaigns provide clear-cut choices between candidates, a great many races involve opponents with only slight differences. In such elections, the better planned and more thoroughly organized campaigns will make the difference between victory and defeat.

I first became acquainted with Loren Belker at church, where we would drink coffee after the service and discuss public affairs. Our friendship deepened as we were both involved in partisan campaigns. He has held most of the major political party offices at a state level.

In 1970 when I first ran for Governor of Nebraska against an incumbent Governor, I asked Loren Belker to be my state-wide campaign chairman. We won that race decisively in what the news media considered a major upset. Loren was again my state chairman when I ran for reelection in 1974, when we won by a bigger margin. When I ran for the United States Senate in 1978, Loren was again at my side. We won that race by an even larger margin, winning ninety-two of the state's ninety-three counties. This is no theoretical approach. He's been there.

Loren Belker is one of the most knowledgeable campaign operatives in the country. Any potential candidate or campaign chairman can benefit from his experience. He not only understands it, he also is able to write about it in an instructive and entertaining way.

J. James Exon,
United States Senator

Preface

THIS BOOK IS ADDRESSED TO candidates, campaign leaders, and volunteers. Hundreds of thousands of people run for office each year. The offices they seek range from city council, village assembly and school board to the United States Congress. The campaign is often derailed from its goal because of the campaign inexperience of either the candidate, the campaign workers, or both. If both the campaign leadership and the candidate are neophytes then the uninitiated are leading the inexperienced.

The better candidate does not always win, but usually the better campaign wins.

This book is intended to provide some insight into the campaign process. I have attempted to write it in such a way that the principles involved are applicable to almost any size campaign. It is not written solely for the person running for office for the first time. It will also be useful to a candidate seeking an office other than the one currently being held.

The reader will find a heavy emphasis in this book on the relationships that exist or should exist between the people in a political campaign. Campaigns become ineffective because of the people problems that are allowed to develop, more than for any other reason. The opposition is the problem, but a candidate cannot effectively deal with the opposition if constant internal problems are diverting everyone's attention.

There are a lot of personal opinions about campaigning in this book, but they are based on my own experiences and are offered for their value to the reader. Those experiences are influenced by my geographic background and some of my comments may not apply to the reader's own geographic area. The reader will have to decide where local custom or tradition requires the modification of some of the principles.

Part I

Basic Organizational Structure

1

The Campaign Chairman

THE CANDIDATE AND THE CAMPAIGN chairman actually select each other. I am covering this selection now as it is usually the first campaign decision the candidate makes. In many situations the person asked to be the campaign chairman has been encouraging the candidate to seek the office. It may have been done very casually. During the course of the discussions about who should run for the office, a statement like this may have been made: "Well, if I do run, you'll have to be my campaign chairman."

If the campaign chairman is chosen in such a casual manner, often the chairman is very close to the candidate. There are advantages and disadvantages to having the candidate and chairman be close friends.

Several advantages come to mind. If they are close friends they have already developed open communication between themselves. There should be no problem with "telling it like it is." Also, they know many of the same people, so that others who are asked to help on the campaign are already known to both. The close friend who is chosen as a chairman already knows how the candidate feels about many issues. The close friend can usually accurately anticipate how the candidate will

3

react to new information or situations based on past knowledge and experience.

The disadvantages include the possibility that if they are too close, the campaign chairman might have a tendency to protect the candidate's feelings instead of telling him what he ought to hear and know. The chairman may assume his candidate-friend is going to react a certain way, when in reality the candidate is now perceiving problems differently than he did when they shared issues over coffee or cocktails. Friendships of many years have been severely tested during the heat of a political campaign. Some have been ripped asunder, never to be mended.

There needs to be a clear understanding between the candidate and the campaign chairman as to which decisions will be made by the candidate and which will be made by the campaign chairman. The candidate obviously will decide which issues he is comfortable with and which he intends to highlight as he seeks the office. The campaign chairman should contribute to this planning process, but the final decisions as to the issue thrust of the campaign should solely be the candidate's. You cannot run a race by a majority vote of the volunteers working on the campaign.

These two people must have a great deal of confidence in each other. If that confidence does not exist, one of them is in the wrong position. The last few weeks of a campaign is an inappropriate time to find out that there is a lack of trust in each other's decision-making ability. The question that needs to be asked is this: "Given the same set of circumstances and information, would both individuals make basically the same decision?" This is not the kind of question that can be tested in advance because you cannot simulate the exact circumstances that are likely to occur in the last stages of a campaign.

A campaign chairman needs to know that the candidate will not fold under pressure, and that he will not compromise his principles when the heat is on.

Conversely, the candidate must be reassured that the campaign chairman will make the correct decisions as they affect the campaign. Late in the campaign the candidate will be so busy with prospective voters that he will have to be able to put organization problems out of his mind. He can do this if he completely supports the campaign chairman's decision-making ability.

Late in a campaign, the candidate is likely to be over-worked, tired and irritable. All the details should be removed from his shoulders at this point so that he can concentrate on the most important part of the campaign — meeting the voter and being highly visible. I will spend more time on this subject later while discussing campaign strategy and the campaign it-self.

As I mentioned earlier, these two people must have the kind of relationship in which complete honesty exists between them. If the candidate wants a campaign chairman who will build his ego and make him feel good about what a savior he is, then he is looking for the wrong traits in a chairman. The campaign chairman must be a first-class truth sender and the candidate must be a first-class truth receiver. The reason is obvious — volunteers will tell a chairman problems that exist with the campaign; they are less likely to tell the candidate. The chairman must be completely free to discuss these matters with the candidate.

I am spending a lot of time on this relationship because it is essential to the success of the campaign. If a chairman has to spend too much of his time filtering news or waiting for the ap-propriate moment to communicate with the candidate, there will be much wasted effort.

You can easily understand why a candidate might want all good news and sweetness and light within his own campaign family. He is out in public campaigning, where he often runs into insults from voters who support the other candidate; he is getting weary from some of the insane questions that he is asked; he is getting tired of the joint appearances with the op-posing candidate; he is beginning to wonder why he ever got into this ridiculous situation. So when he comes back home to his campaign headquarters, he expects to find warmth, safety, and approval.

I am not suggesting that a campaign chairman has no need for discretion in dealing with the candidate. He should not hit a candidate across the mouth with some bad news at an inappropriate time if it can be avoided; but when it is necessary, the campaign chairman must have the courage to communicate it.

I think it is best if the campaign chairman is an individual who does not want a job with the candidate when that victorious candidate becomes an office holder. This, of course, assumes that he wins the kind of office where the authority to hire staff people does exist. If the campaign chairman does not want a job with the office holder, I believe he can maintain his objectivity much more easily. He is not "beholden" in advance. There is a greater temptation to protect your flanks if there is a job waiting in the wings.

It could be argued that if the campaign chairman is going to take a job with the office holder, he has a deep personal stake in the results of the campaign and he will work that much harder. I believe it is not a matter of working "harder" but "smarter" that is important. I personally lean toward a campaign chairman who does not plan on taking a job; it gives him an independence that I think is important.

The campaign chairman should be an individual who has had some political experience. He doesn't have to have chaired a campaign before, but he should be an individual who has been associated with a previous political effort. It also helps if the chairman has some management or administrative experience. A political campaign is a management situation requiring administrative skills. Almost all parts of a political campaign can be broken down into management functions.

The campaign chairman must know something about leadership. He must know how to direct people in tasks that they are to perform. If this individual has not had much leadership experience, then he ought to read a basic book on the management of people. (If it does not appear too crass and commercial, may I suggest my book *The First Time Manager*, published 1979 by Ama-Com, a division of the American Management Associations of New York City.)

There will be campaign committee meetings and a chairman must have the skills of a successful meeting leader. Too many political meetings last longer than they should because they wander away from the appointed task. There is a temptation for a political committee to review the entire campaign at every meeting.

The chairman should prepare an agenda before every meeting and hold to that agenda. Of course, he may move away from the agenda for emergency matters. He should schedule both beginning and ending times for meetings; more meetings would be conducted with dispatch and efficiency if they were restricted to specific time frames. If the committee is not finished with the agenda at the appointed time, unfinished items can be taken up at the next meeting. The chairman must be committed to the appointed finishing time, or the attendees at the meeting will know it is a meaningless gesture. I honestly believe that you could get more people to serve on committees if they know a meeting is going to last one hour than if they suspect it may shoot the entire evening.

A campaign chairman must be an individual who can subject his own ego to that of the candidate. The chairman cannot be in competition with the candidate for recognition, even among those closest to the campaign. He must be willing to constantly build up that candidate. If he cannot willingly accept this "number two" role, then he ought to be a candidate rather than a campaign chairman. The campaign chairman is not the box at the top of the organization chart. That spot is reserved for the candidate. The chairman must be willing to accept the next slot down.

Many a successful office holder was at one time a campaign chairman for someone else. The experience of running someone else's campaign is a valuable one for anyone running for political office. It is during such an experience that the "bug" may bite the chairman. I doubt if there has ever been a campaign chairman who did not at least once think, "Maybe someday I'll run for office myself." Decisions will be made by a candidate during a campaign that a chairman would not have made, and so the thought occasionally surfaces about "how I'd do it, if I ever ran for office."

A candidate should be a strong person and a chairman should have the same quality. These two are not always going to agree, but in the final analysis it is the candidate who is running and his position must prevail. Hopefully, disagreements between the two can be handled privately, and not in front of the entire campaign committee.

A campaign chairman does not sign up forever, and he does not sign up "no matter what," and that is why sometimes during the heat of the campaign, the chairman resigns and is replaced. The situation usually could have been avoided if the two involved knew and understood each other well.

There is no candidate, no office, no campaign, no potential political appointment more important than personal integrity. If a campaign chairman feels that to continue he must compromise his principles, then he should get out. That candidate does not deserve him. It should not become necessary if the candidate and the situation are thoroughly understood before taking on the job.

One of the mixed blessings of conducting a successful campaign is that you get the reputation of an instant political expert. Go ahead and enjoy it, but don't believe it. There are no experts, including the political science professors in major universities. Most of the so-called experts are merely students who have learned a little more than some other students.

Politics is similar to advertising and public relations in that everyone in the field thinks he is an expert. As a result no one is. The people I know who have been most successful in politics or in managing campaigns do not consider themselves experts. They would not deny that title if you insisted on giving it

to them, but they will privately admit what they really are —
avid students of the art.

There is a great satisfaction to successfully chairing a campaign. Unlike many of life's activities, you do not have to wonder how you did. You will know when those votes are counted.

2

The Treasurer

THE CASUAL HANDLING OF MONEY in political campaigns is a thing of the past in most parts of the country. Federal offices now come under the regulations of the Federal Election Commission. Many states have passed various "sunshine" and disclosure laws that regulate state campaigns; communities have municipal ordinances that apply to local campaigns and elections.

While many people active in the political process feel that this legal action has gone overboard, the fact is that a much greater need exists now for the accountability of campaign contributions than existed a few years ago. The openness of political contributions is a healthy advancement for the political process in America.

I cannot spell out specific requirements in this chapter because what is applicable in my state may not apply to your local situation at all. So any recommendations must be general in nature.

A treasurer should not be selected on the basis of whether or not he would be a good fund raiser. The person who has the ability to go out and seek contributions can be the finance chairman. Too many candidates feel that the qualities of a treasurer and fund raiser must be combined in one person. If such an individual is willing to accept both responsibilities, there is nothing to preclude such an arrangement. However, there is some advantage to having the duties handled by two different people.

The most obvious advantage is the independent check and balance procedures that can be established. The campaign committee, on the advice of legal counsel or an accountant, can establish the ground rules for the contributions that can be accepted. I will address this in more detail in the chapter on fund raising.

In a large campaign there are likely to be a multitude of contributions coming from a wide geographic area. Obviously, there are many advantages to having the books audited and the proper reporting done by a certified public accounting firm. This should be done on a regular payment basis. It means that the campaign books and reports will be handled on a professional level. The accounting firm should not be expected to donate the service.

If a candidate cannot or does not want to use a C.P.A. firm for auditing and reporting, then the very least he should do is have a treasurer who knows something about keeping a simple set of books, and who can properly prepare reports. This person should have a great eye for detail; this is one area where a perfectionist comes in very handy. Someone who figures, "if it gets within a couple of bucks, that's close enough," won't do. A number of years ago, that kind of attitude was quite common, but with the current laws and regulations, such an approach cannot be accepted. Hopefully, those connected with a campaign effort will be people of integrity, but it is absolutely mandatory with the people handling the money and the books. A treasurer should not bend the rules even if the candidate asks for a shortcut to be taken here or there. A discussion with the potential treasurer should be held before campaign planning begins, so that the individual fully understands that the backing of the candidate and the chairman will be there if ever anyone suggests that there be compromises concerning the books, payment of bills, or reporting.

It is essential that the treasurer have some basic knowledge about keeping a set of books. He or she should at least know the difference between a debit and a credit beyond knowing that "the debits go next to the window."

The treasurer should attend all campaign meetings, because much that will be decided at such meetings will be influenced by the financial status of the campaign. Too often, those working on a campaign who have no responsibility for raising money are very free to make recommendations that will deplete the financial resources of the committee. People have their own little theories about what constitutes the most effective campaigning. I have known people who sincerely believed that a campaign was doomed to failure if a large percentage of the resources were not poured into matchbook advertising. The treasurer is the proper person to consult concerning the cost effectiveness of various campaign expenses. The area where the treasurer might have difficulty is with financing the pet projects of the candidate and the chairman. Although these two people have the authority to make such decisions, it still is a sound business practice for the treasurer to question all expenditures.

Nearly all campaigns have limited resources. Priorities must be established, and the treasurer can be very effective in this regard. He can make certain that the campaign is not obligating itself for money it does not have or is not likely to have. To some people on the campaign committee the treasurer becomes the "bastard at the family picnic." He must be willing to play this role if he is to be effective. He should be cooperative without being a patsy.

The treasurer should also be familiar with the state or city campaign laws, or whatever regulations apply to the particular race. Even if an accounting firm is used for maintaining the books, a treasurer who does not know the rules can get the campaign into trouble. Let us say that for your particular race, it is illegal to accept a corporate check. If a corporate check comes in and the treasurer deposits it in the checking account, the damage could be done. It could happen quite innocently. If at a later time a campaign check is written to refund the illegal contribution, it still does not solve the problem. Your opposition could accuse you of accepting an illegal campaign contribution. The chances are that you would have to report both the receipt and the return of the gift. Even though it may or may not be a technical violation, it could cause some serious problems for the campaign. Voters who do not take the trouble to find out the facts may not see beyond the charge of receipt of an illegal campaign contribution. Elections have been lost on such minor matters.

Every campaign should have a second person who is also authorized to sign campaign checks; often this is an assistant treasurer. There does not have to be an assistant treasurer, but there does need to be someone else on the campaign committee who can sign checks in the absence of the treasurer. In some campaigns the chairman will be the second person who can sign checks. This prevents a situation where the emergency illness of the treasurer would bring the campaign to a grinding halt.

Campaigns have been known to have checking accounts in which all checks require the signatures of two people. Circumstances will dictate whether or not this is an acceptable method of operation. The larger the operation, the more likely it is that this procedure be used.

A modified version of this two-signature approach would require two signatures on checks for more than a certain amount. Many banks are reluctant to go along with this kind of arrangement because of the additional processing work. However, it is worth inquiring about.

Even though banks may have a service charge arrangement for checking accounts, many will offer a service-free account to a political campaign. It may not be offered, so the treasurer should ask for it. There is no sense in spending a cent of those hard-to-come-by contributions if it is unnecessary. This same free service does not usually apply to the printing of the checks themselves. The checks must be paid for by somebody and under the laws governing some campaigns, this would have to be reported as an "in-kind"* contribution if the bank were to donate them.

The selection of a treasurer is an important decision to be made very early in the campaign and it should not be made without proper consideration of the duties that will be required of that individual.

---

*A contribution of goods or services, rather than one in money.

3

Other Campaign Staff

IN ADDITION TO THE CANDIDATE, the chairman, and the treasurer, other campaign staff members may be needed. Like so many facets of a political campaign, the number of people will depend on the kind of campaign being organized. I will discuss both paid and volunteer staffing.

One or two full-time staff people will help nearly any campaign if the money is there to fund them. For the sake of organizing this chapter, let's assume that there will be a full-time paid executive director and secretary and that the chairman and the treasurer are volunteers.

A general job description for a campaign executive director is helpful unless the individual has been involved in a political campaign before and knows just what is expected and it is clearly understood by the candidate, the chairman, and the director.

If a paid staff exists then there must be a place for the staff to work, so one of the first duties of an executive director may be to obtain office space. The director may locate various possibilities, but the final decision on space to be rented will usually be made by the chairman or the candidate. Often a premium will be paid for space since rental will last for only a short term.

The second decision to be made concerns the rental of furniture and other equipment for the office. Since a campaign is a short-term project, only temporary equipment is needed to get the job done. It's best to shop around for the rental of furniture and equipment, as some distributors try to overcharge campaigns, recognizing that they do not have much choice. Again, if someone offers to donate the use of equipment or furniture, the reporting requirements should be checked. It may be that a corporation cannot loan the equipment because it represents a corporate contribution, even though it is an "in-kind" contribution. (I cannot help but feel that those people who oppose corporate campaign contributions are corporation officers who want a legal excuse for not helping. Before such laws they had to choose which candidates to help; under the laws they no longer have to make such judgments.)

The candidate may be able to loan items such as a desk or typewriter out of his own home that can be used in the office. Here again they may have to be reported as in-kind contributions.

Another early job responsibility of an executive director is the hiring of a combination secretary-receptionist-office clerk. One of the prime prerequisites of this job is handling and meeting the public. This must be a person with a pleasant and friendly telephone voice who genuinely likes meeting and working with people. This must be a sincere attitude—it cannot be faked. This combination secretary-receptionist-office clerk will often be the first person that the public will come in contact with either in person or by phone. The first and often lasting impression that people will receive will be formed by this contact. Of course this person should also possess the necessary office skills.

I think it is a sound idea for the executive director to ask the candidate and the chairman to okay the person selected for the secretarial position. There is no sense in having the candidate or chairman annoyed every time he calls the office.

One reason one cannot be exactly precise about job duties or a job description is that in a political campaign the paid staff cannot worry about an exact delineation of duties. Many people enjoy the challenge, excitement, and turmoil of a campaign. People who do enjoy it do not worry too much about who is responsible for what, and they make outstanding staff members.

Promises, Promises

I have already made reference to the relationship of the chairman to the candidate and vice versa. Again, I do not believe it is a good idea for the candidate to promise staff people jobs if he or she is elected. If a staff member is promised a position and then does not perform up to expectation, the candidate has a real problem in breaking what the staff person believes is a commitment. There are times in political campaigns when some staff people do not perform as expected but are kept on board, for political reasons. A disgruntled fired employee can do a campaign a lot of damage by giving inside information to the opponent. If an unsatisfactory performer is kept on the campaign staff, there is a problem in finding him a job when the candidate takes office.

If people on the campaign staff do an outstanding job, the candidate can always offer them a position after the election. It is best not to be so encumbered. The outstanding performer will not be worried about whether or not he is promised a job. He knows that the possibility is there, and usually feels if measured on performance, he will do all right.

Many candidates running for part-time offices do not have this problem because they have no jobs to offer. By the same token, they usually will not put on full-time campaign staffs. If a full-time staff is needed once elected, then a full-time staff may very well be needed to win the office.

The Rest of the Organization

The balance of the organization is staffed by volunteers. What is discussed here about volunteers will tie in with the chapter on "The Care and Feeding of Volunteers."

One of the primary functions of the executive director is to secure an adequate number of volunteers to assist with the campaign and insure political victory.

Some of the sources for campaign volunteers are as follows: friends of the candidate, chairman, and executive director; workers from previous campaigns, from the political party, from Young Republicans or Young Democrats, or from interest groups who share similar views to the candidate; students; League of Women Voters members (if the race is nonpartisan); workers from voter registration lists; and political contributors.

There will be people who volunteer to help with a campaign shortly after the candidate announces that he will run. These names should be jotted down and given to the chairman or the executive director.

An experienced candidate or a campaign chairman may be surprised to know that people may volunteer, and then when called upon will be disappointing in their lack of response.

There are many people who are absolutely outstanding when it comes to talking about a campaign, but who will never perform when the chips are down. It's good to know that from the outset. If a candidate were to ask a group of people to attend a meeting on campaign strategy, he will draw a much larger crowd than he would if he called a meeting about going door to door with campaign brochures.

However, it is my opinion that only those who have paid their dues should be discussing campaign strategy. I do not believe people should be deciding on various campaign activities unless they have performed most of those activities themselves at one time or another. If the staff is all new, then that ideal situation is not possible; then I believe the candidate and the chairman should also participate in these activities. It gives them some valuable experience and it is good for the morale of the volunteers to see the leadership willing to get out and do what they are being asked to do.

Span of Control

One reason a lot of campaigns fail is improper organization. When analyzing their organizational structure, it becomes clear that such campaigns violate one basic organizational principle called "span of control."

The span of control concept is violated when too many workers report to one person. Some theories say that a proper span of control exists when you have from six to ten people reporting to one individual; this size is manageable. Some campaigns have had as many as thirty or forty people reporting to the same individual. This kind of situation breaks down especially when there is a lot to do in the late days of a campaign. It is repaired in a haphazard way to try to get the job accomplished. It could be avoided by using proper management theories in the beginning.

Another advantage in having this limited number of people reporting to one person is that they get to know each other well. The leader of a group such as this learns the strengths and weaknesses of his people and has the opportunity to build some *esprit de corps* among the group.

This span of control concept should be followed throughout the organization from the chairman down to the precinct captain. While the chairman is directing only a limited number of people, he does not need to concern himself with the personal direction of all the people.

One reason many people ignore this span of control concept is that they see too many layers between the top and the bottom. They fear that too many layers will create too much insulation or such a cumbersome organization that it will take far too long for communications to filter up and down the organization. This is a legitimate concern until you consider the chaos that results when you ignore this approach. The way to solve the problem is to work on the streamlining and the expediting of communication approaches rather than to ignore basic principles that have been proven to be beneficial through years of managerial experience.

By looking at the sample organization chart (see Figure 3.1), you can see that there are four layers of communication from the chairman to the block captain. A fairly large organization is shown in this sample. Many campaign structures would not need to be this elaborate; a few would need to be even more complete. I think the chart illustrates the point about layers of communication.

Setting Up an Office

Some campaigns can be run out of the home of the candidate and do not require a campaign headquarters as such. However, many campaigns do have need for an office.

Obviously, a campaign headquarters is not going to need a long-term lease. An office may be needed anywhere from a few weeks to one year.

One factor to consider is whether or not an office with street level visibility is needed. Depending on the real estate situation in the community, usually such a visible office will cost more to rent than space buried inside some office building.

There are both advantages and disadvantages to a street level office. Some of the advantages are:

1. If the office is in a great location, everyone going by is reminded of the candidacy being promoted. It is, in essence, a campaign billboard.

2. If it is a location where there is a lot of foot traffic, it is easy for people to come in and pick up campaign materials.

3. If there is a lot of activity in the office, it adds to the positive image of the campaign.

4. A good looking operation may attract volunteers.
Some of the disadvantages are:

1. The office must be staffed at all times. The closed or apparently inactive office may cause some people to think the campaign is in difficulty.

2. The office gets a lot of nuisance traffic. Campaign button collectors come in and want material.

3. There is a chance that people from the opposition may come in and ask for material with the express purpose of throwing it away. This type of mischief does take place.

4. There may be ordinance limitations on what can be done in the way of advertising.

If this type of office is chosen, be sure that there is adequate parking, primarily for volunteers who may come to the headquarters to make phone calls, stuff envelopes, or do other campaign work. Parking for staff members is not as critical because there are usually only a few of them. But if fifteen or twenty people arrive some evening to address envelopes and there is no free or low-cost parking close to the office, it will be difficult to get them back again.

When considering a prospective office of this type, look it over at night. How is a volunteer going to feel coming to or leaving the headquarters at night? Is it safe? Is it properly lit? Is there difficulty in the neighborhood? Is it a high crime area?

Another factor to think about in considering a street level location is the rent. The reaction to a campaign's need for space can be at both extremes—as a short-term tenant, the landlord may try to overcharge for campaign headquarters; or if the owner is favorable to the campaign, the office may be offered at a reduced rate or rent-free. (If this happens do not overlook the fact that there may be an in-kind campaign contribution to be reported.)

If the rent is too high, consider renting space in an office building. In this situation the location may not be nearly as critical because you are not considered with visibility; the observations about parking and safety still apply however. Often you can rent an office somewhere, buy a billboard at a highly visible corner, and achieve the effect of a visible office at less expense.

Once a location is decided on and a deal is struck with the

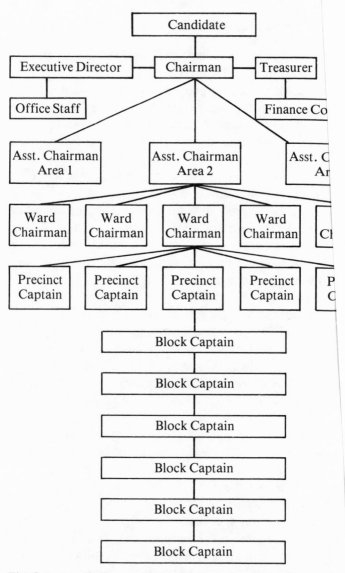

Fig. 3.1. A typical organizational chart that recognizes the "spa
control" concept with only one complete channel shown from t
bottom for illustration purposes. Note: The entire organiza
shown under Assistant Chairman Area 2 also exists under Assis
Chairman Areas 1 and 3.

management, there are other decisions to be made before opening an office.

Do not buy furniture. It will cost too much and end up being virtually given away when the campaign is over. The rule goes basically like this: "When a campaign wants to buy furniture, it is a seller's market. When a campaign wants to sell furniture, it is a buyer's market." It will always be so!

Someone sympathetic to the campaign may have office furniture to lend. (Again, pay attention to campaign reporting laws.) Or perhaps it can be rented at a reasonable fee. The office does not need furniture that looks like an executive suite, just serviceable equipment — comfortable chairs are more important than the style of the desks. The office will not need a lot of desks. Tables will do just as well.

Often typewriters and other office equipment can be leased. The advantage of leasing is that most lease agreements include servicing of the equipment. If a piece of machinery is a constant service problem, the lessor will often replace it rather than go to the expense of constant service calls to the campaign headquarters.

Telephones must be given very serious consideration. In most campaigns more equipment is installed than is needed, and the monthly service charges use up campaign capital that could be used for other efforts. Very often, the heavy telephone use will take place in the last six weeks of the campaign. It's preferable to wait to put the phones in until the time they are needed. A good campaign rule is "never buy it until you need it," assuming it will be available then.

If this is a local community campaign, phones for local use only can be installed. Some telephone companies in some locations in the country can provide a service that interrupts anyone attempting to make a long distance call, and informs the caller that a long distance call cannot be made on that phone. This procedure can save the cost of unauthorized long distance calls.

Many a political campaign has ended up paying for or being billed for thousands of dollars of unauthorized phone calls. In most jurisdictions that I am familiar with, if it is your phone and the calls were made on that instrument, you are liable for the phone calls.

Unauthorized phone calls can be controlled even if long distance calls are used as a part of the campaign. Use a telephone log. Everyone on the staff who *is authorized* to make long distance phone calls on behalf of the campaign should record the date of the call, the person and town called, and the approximate time used. When the monthly billing comes in, it should be checked against the log and there should be a discussion among the staff to explain any discrepancies. This type of record keeping is very beneficial.

Telephone locks can be purchased for a very modest amount. These locks make it impossible to dial the phone and, obviously, to make long distance calls. These devices protect the phones from unauthorized use after hours or during the periods when someone from the staff cannot be present.

In many parts of the country, telephone companies require substantial deposits from political campaigns before they will even install phones. Frankly, I don't blame them. Telephone companies across the country have millions of dollars of unpaid phone bills from political campaigns ranging from presidential campaigns down to school boards. Winning campaigns are easier to collect from than losing ones, because winning candidates become office holders. Many phone companies require personal guarantees from the candidate or another person connected with the campaign that the statement will be paid.

If the campaign will be using the telephone extensively for long distance, look into the feasibility of a WATS (Wide Area Tele-Communication System) line. A flat fee covers all phone calls made within the state. Do a very thorough and realistic estimate of how much long distance will be used. In most campaigns WATS lines are installed because the workers are fascinated with the concept. If they would do a realistic cost-benefit ratio study, they would find that they could not justify a WATS line. Do a realistic study before making such a decision.

There are many long distance calls made in political campaigns that need never be made. Staff members are intrigued with the idea of picking up the phone and calling a volunteer in another part of the state. Too often it is an ego trip. Such attitudes cost campaigns money that should never be spent. This is one of the values of a budget (covered in another chapter) — it lets everyone know that there is an expected restraint on such expenses.

4

The Care and Feeding
of Volunteers

ONE OF THE PRIMARY INGREDIENTS of a successful campaign
is the efficient recruitment and use of volunteers.

A complaint made more often by volunteers than any other
is, "I offered to help, but it was weeks before anyone asked me
to do anything," or "I volunteered my services, but no one ever
called me."

It is strange that one of the primary complaints of volunteers is that their free services were not fully utilized or not
called upon at all. I do not believe that this happens because
volunteers are not needed; it is primarily a matter of timing
and communication. People may volunteer very early in a
campaign at a time when the strategy has yet to be determined.
In many campaigns a heavy concentration of activity is
planned for relatively short periods of time, such as six weeks
before either the primary and general election. If the campaign
committee makes a decision to start heavy activity around Labor Day, an individual who volunteers his services in June will
probably be so disenchanted when the call for work goes out
the middle of August that he will tell the campaign coordinator to "stick it in your ear."

The solution to this problem is to let people know when

their services will be needed at the time they volunteer or are recruited. If they know what activities are planned it will help solidify them in the campaign. They feel that they have "inside information" that outsiders do not have. Everyone needs to feel that they are special and this is vitally important with volunteers.

If there is one cardinal rule that must be observed in dealing with volunteers it is this: "Volunteers are not employees. The employer–employee relationship does not exist." Volunteers are with a campaign for a variety of reasons, not all of which are unselfish.

Some volunteers like the excitement of a campaign; they find it an exhilarating experience. Others like rubbing elbows with candidates and office holders. Some hope that there may be a political job or appointment for them if the campaign is successful. Still others want the opportunity to be able to talk to the office holder about their pet project or issue, and it is easier to talk with friends than it is with enemies. Some are relatives or friends of the candidate, or friends of a friend. Believe it or not, there still are some who volunteer because they believe in the American political process and feel a commitment to participate.

In the chapter that dealt with staff and promises I strongly recommended that no commitments be made for jobs after the election. The candidate must take a similar position as it relates to issues and volunteers. But this gets complicated because it may be the office seeker's position on an issue that attracts the volunteer's support in the first place. That is a part of the political process and is to be expected. If a volunteer is attracted to a candidate because of his position on taxes and spending, that is a philosophy that can be consistently maintained. The kind of situation that is fraught with danger exists when the volunteer expects the candidate to vote, for example, for zoning in which the volunteer has a financial interest, in return for the volunteer's contribution and work. If a candidate makes deals like this, he or she is committed to a position that may not be acceptable once all sides of the question are known. Even if the candidate independently arrives at the same position on such an issue, casting that decision in concrete in return for support makes that office holder "beholden" and less of a public servant than he or she could otherwise be. The office holders cannot change their minds if they have prostituted themselves in return for a campaign contribution or other kind of support.

I think a contributor or volunteer has the right to expect that the candidate attempt to be the best office holder possible. Of course people are going to support candidates who think the way they would under the same set of circumstances. It is this kind of philosophical meeting of the minds that attracts support to a candidate in the first place.

There are candidates who promise anything to anybody in return for votes. Some of these people do get elected and then find themselves caught in a cross fire of contradictory support and positions that they cannot live with. To get out of such situations they compromise future positions and become political puppets ruled by the cross current of fickle political winds.

Often the little things done by a candidate or the campaign committee can solidify the volunteer with the campaign. For example, the candidate can have a letter sent to all volunteers thanking them for offering their help. It's best if this type of letter is personally signed by the candidate. A preprinted form letter with a reproduction of the candidate's signature is, in my opinion, worse than no acknowledgment. It says that the candidate does not care enough to even sign the letter, and usually generates a very negative response from the volunteer. Of course the letters can be prepared in the campaign office and there may be a "sample letter" that is individually typed or prepared from a tape. But the personalized signature of the candidate should appear on all letters.

In some campaigns volunteers are sent photos of the candidate, sometimes at the time the individual volunteers. That is much too early. The fact that a person volunteers does not mean that he will actually do any work. Some volunteers will decide they do not like any of the tasks they are asked to perform. If photos are sent early in the campaign, there may be so many of them floating around that they become meaningless.

The photograph idea makes more sense after the campaign is over and the candidate has won. Then the photo going to people who really helped becomes meaningful. A personal inscription by the candidate is more meaningful. Photographs should be eight by ten inches or no smaller than five by seven, and can be printed with an inch of white space at the bottom, providing an ideal place for the inscription.

If a candidate loses the election, I think sending out photographs is less meaningful. Volunteers still should be thanked, but I think a personal letter is more meaningful. Let's face it — people do not display pictures of candidates who lose. As soon as you win, the photo goes up.

It is a good idea to plan on keeping the campaign office open for a few days or weeks after the election to take care of some of these personal touches. There is nothing worse, in my opinion, than failing to express appreciation to volunteers after a losing campaign. I know of dedicated volunteers who refused to work on a candidate's campaign because there were no thanks expressed after a previous losing effort. No matter how much that loss hurts the candidate, it hurts the campaign workers too, and to fail to thank them is a very self-centered reaction.

When people volunteer to help on a campaign, some inquiries should be made about them. There are people who should not be associated with a campaign. A candidate would not want a known criminal working on his election effort. That kind of help can kill a campaign. A candidate may not want people to volunteer who have taken a position on an issue that is an embarrassment to him. For example, if a losing candidate for city council who advocated the legalization of prostitution speaks out publicly for you, it could cost you votes. If a person like that really wants to help, you are better off with his silent support.

I attended a political dinner for presidential candidates in

1968. Among those in attendance were Sam Yorty, Robert Kennedy, and Hubert Humphrey. Unable to attend was then Vice-President Humphrey's fellow Minnesotan Eugene Mc-Carthy. When the vice-president got up to make his speech as reported in the *Nebraska Jefferson-Jackson Day Dinner,* he said, "I'm sorry Gene couldn't be here, but I've sent him a tele-gram in which I asked him if he considered it in his best interest if I speak for him or against him."

The point is that there are some people in the community whose help a candidate does not want because of what it can do to his campaign. He should not immediately accept every offer of help. A candidate should tailor his attitude to his local conditions.

Key people in the campaign must be responsible citizens. A candidate cannot have people associated with his campaign who lose him votes everywhere they go. An individual who writes insufficient funds checks all over town is not the person he wants wearing one of his campaign buttons.

Of course, a retail credit report cannot be run on everyone who works on a campaign, but there should be a method of checking into a person's general reputation before he is given a responsible position with the campaign. The headline "Smith's Campaign Treasurer Booked in Gambling Raid" will not help Smith win elections. A candidate cannot control every possi-ble situation that may develop. You could have an individual going door to door in a precinct who could be so unpopular in the neighborhood that he will cost the campaign votes. The ef-fort would be better off with no one going door to door than with such a negative person. All he can do is make sure that those who are recruiting people are sensitive to the fact that only reputable citizens should be associated with the cam-paign.

Occasionally volunteers will get so caught up with the idea of winning a campaign that they will stoop to almost any level to win. I have heard of volunteers who go to the opposition's headquarters and pick up as much campaign material as they can with the express purpose of throwing it away once they get outside. Another example is the destroying of the opponent's political signs. This destruction is illegal and has no place in ethical political campaigns. The leadership must set the tone of the campaign. The candidate and the chairman have to make it clear from the outset that they are running hard, but that they are running a fair and equitable campaign. A candidate who will tolerate dirty tricks during the campaign will also cut corners as an office holder. Unfortunately there are people who view dirty tricks as the Halloween "fun and games" of politics. I think it is important that the candidate become the office holder with absolutely no misgivings as to how he got there.

Sometimes there is a pretty thin line between what is hard, tough campaigning and what is hitting below the belt. I think having letters written to the editor of a newspaper extolling the candidate and criticizing the opponent's position is hard, tough campaigning. Starting a whispering campaign about the drinking problem of the opponent's spouse, even if true, is hitting below the belt.

Having volunteers phone in tough questions to a "call in" radio show featuring the opponent to answer is hard, tough campaigning. Asking him questions which deliberately distort his position is hitting below the belt.

Sending workers wearing campaign buttons to an open public rally of the opponent may be tough, hard campaigning (even though I do not recommend it). Disrupting the opponent's rally is hitting below the belt.

It is important that volunteers coming to the campaign understand their responsibilities, but more importantly, the limit of their authority.

5

The Policy Committee

THE POLICY COMMITTEE COULD ALSO be classified as an advisory committee because any decisions that it makes are in fact advisory to the candidate. The committee cannot make any policy that the candidate will not accept.

This committee should consist of the chairman, the treasurer, the finance chairman, the executive director, and several other at-large members selected because of their background and past experience, their knowledge of the community, or general campaign experience.

It is helpful to have some at-large members on the policy committee because they can bring some perspective to the campaign that people who are involved on a day-to-day basis may miss. These at-large members, if they are selected for their objectivity, can feed back to the campaign committee the community's reactions to the campaign and the candidate.

The policy committee should meet with some degree of regularity, but not too often, if it is to be of any assistance to the campaign. It is tempting to call a meeting every time a problem comes up, but the policy committee should not meet to discuss minute items that can be decided by the chairman, executive director, or the candidate.

As discussed in a previous chapter, there needs to be a concise attitude toward these policy committee meetings. I think more is accomplished in an hour meeting than in one that is allowed to drift on and on. The people who are on this committee are usually busy people who will appreciate a businesslike approach to the meetings. There is a great temptation to make every meeting a reevaluation of the campaign strategy. Many campaigns become losers because such frequent changes in direction result in a campaign that drifts aimlessly. Once you determine your game plan, stick with it for a reasonable length of time. If you correctly analyze the objective and the method to achieve it, you cannot move away from it every time a little problem comes up. I hesitantly use a football analogy (because I am just a fan and not an expert on the game): if the opposition scores a quick fluke touchdown in the first quarter, you do not immediately abandon your game plan and start playing desperation ball. If your game plan is sound you stick with it; a change of game plan is not likely to provide an answer. Your plan should be a plan of action, not a plan of reaction.

The campaign chairman ought to function as the chairman of the policy committee. He may turn the chair over to others when it comes to their areas of responsibility.

Let's look at an agenda for a typical advisory committee:

1. Report from the executive director
   (a) recruitment of volunteers
   (b) telephone campaign
2. Report on media buys — chairman
3. Report from treasurer
   (a) financial report
4. Report from finance chairman
5. Discussion of reaction to opponent's charge that our candidate lacks administrative experience
6. Report from candidate
7. Scheduling of next meeting
8. Adjournment

It may occur to the reader that some of these agenda items are rather routine, but all aspects of a campaign must tie into one cohesive unit. The campaign organization should help win the election, not get in the way of the objective.

I think it is valuable for the executive director to have to report his activities to a full committee rather than work directly with the chairman. The chairman cannot be all things to all people—he may have his blind sides. Consequently questions may be addressed to the executive director from other members of the committee that a chairman might not ask. In addition if the chairman runs a good, concise, productive meeting it will set the tone for the meeting that the executive director will schedule with volunteers.

The chairman could report on most any activity. The item I selected happens to be a report on previous decisions about the purchase of various ads on radio and television in the last six weeks of the campaign. He could report on the culmination of any other committee decision.

On item three, the treasurer could give a report on the current financial situation. He might present formal financial statements, or it might be as informal as telling everyone how much money is in the bank and what expenses are outstanding and need to be paid.

On item four, the finance chairman could report on the fund-raising drive. He might report on the finance committee's decision to have a fund-raising dinner for the candidate. A general discussion might follow concerning some of the finance committee's recommendations.

Item five could be one that takes considerable discussion. In this situation the committee would analyze the charge that the opponent is making. Does it have any substance? This is not the time to con each other. If our candidate does not have the administrative experience, how do we handle this charge? Is anybody paying any attention to the charge? If not should we ignore it? Will we help the opponent spread the charge by answering it? This can lead to a rather lengthy discussion. This is the part of politics that many people find the most fun, because it's like a chess game. In this case, the committee, after some discussion, could decide to turn the charge into a plus by suggesting the following approach to the candidate: "I admit I lack the administrative experience that the incumbent has on the job. However, this position requires sound judgment. The voters will have to decide whether they want to continue the administrative experience that has led to the shambles that we find that office in today. I suggest that the voters want and need a fresh approach to the job, one that is not locked to the administrative mistakes of the past four years. The question is not experience. The question is judgment and integrity."

Item six, the report from the candidate, may be most anything. He could review his campaign tactics since the last meeting or bring up items that he wants to bounce off the entire committee.

Item seven may not be necessary if meetings are regularly scheduled.

At a very early campaign meeting the entire plan of the campaign might be discussed. That meeting was not used as a sample, because there might be just one item on the agenda. That could be quite a free-wheeling event, with very little structure.

One caution about a policy or advisory committee: Do not put such a committee together if, as the candidate, you do not really want much advice. I have seen policy committee meetings during which the candidate quarrels or disputes every bit of advice that is offered. It does not take long before such advisors stop coming to meetings. A candidate needs to give serious consideration to the purpose of this committee before putting it together. The committee should consist of people whom the candidate will listen to. Some people just do not have the experience to make them solid advisors for a political campaign.

This is an area where the "palace guard syndrome" cannot be allowed to exist. If individuals on such a committee are only going to tell the candidate what they think he wants to hear, then they are useless except to feed the candidate's ego. That seldom is necessary as most candidates have enough ego to cover the whole committee.

6

The Finance Committee

IN THIS BRIEF CHAPTER I am going to address myself to the finance committee. I am concerned primarily with the organizational makeup of the group. How it functions in its vital role of fund raising will be covered in another section of the book.

The chairman of the finance committee is not necessarily the treasurer. As has been pointed out in the chapter on the treasurer, the chairman of the finance committee is an individual who can accept the responsibility for seeing that the money needed by the campaign is raised. That does not mean that he personally raises all of it, but he does direct the generation of the necessary income.

One of the first questions that comes up when the chairmanship of the finance committee is discussed is whether the individual must be a person of substance. There are conflicting viewpoints on this topic. We will discuss some of the pros and cons; the reader can decide what is applicable to his campaign and its requirements.

One viewpoint is that a finance chairman cannot solicit large contributions if he or she is incapable of making a large contribution. The opposite position is that the job of being a finance chairman is primarily one of organizing the managerial functions that need to be accomplished; as long as he or she can get people to assist who have the rapport with the so-called big givers, that's all that is required.

Another argument is that if a finance chairman is a person of financial substance, the very announcement of that individual to the position will be a prestige event for the campaign. The opposite point of view is that the vast majority of the electorate are not moneyed people. As a result the rank-and-file voter may be turned off by such an announcement and will reason that the candidate has been captured by the "establishment" of the community (whatever that is).

Each community has a power structure of some sort, and an assessment needs to be made as to how a campaign is going to relate to that power structure. Will the campaign run with it, against it, or somewhere in between? The selection of a finance chairman may be determined by the answer to that question. A candidate may decide to play it down the middle and select some middle-class person who can communicate with the big givers, but who is not so identified with them that he or she loses votes with the rank-and-file. Many individuals who are of the power structure of a community believe that they are beloved in the area, because of all the positive things they do. That is not always the case. My purpose is not to attempt to identify all the feelings that may exist in a community, but only to suggest that a candidate pay attention to them as he selects a finance chairman.

The finance chairman and the treasurer must be compatible because they will work closely together on the budget. The finance chairman needs to know what the cash flow requirements are and when certain bills must be paid.

Another quality the finance chairman should possess is the ability to know what kind of contribution people can make. He should not be asking people to contribute $100 who are capable of giving $1,000. The same situation applies to asking individuals to give ten dollars who could give $100.

These are some of the factors to be considered when selecting a finance chairman. This selection could be as important as that of the campaign chairman.

7

The Relationship of the Candidate to the Organization

IN ALL OF THE PRECEDING chapters I have laid heavy emphasis on the personal relationships that need to exist between the people on a campaign. Therefore, I apologize to the reader if some of the points made in this chapter sound redundant. However, it is my opinion that many campaigns get into big difficulty because of the people problems that crop up among those working on the campaigns.

Campaign chairmen have quit in a huff. Volunteers have left one campaign and gone to work for the opposition. People have only half-heartedly performed their duties because of some personal miff they have felt. There is no guarantee that this kind of problem will never crop up in a campaign, but its possibility can be minimized by being aware of it and trying to establish the correct kind of relationship between all of the people involved.

The candidate is the focal point of the campaign, so his relationship with the people on the campaign is more important than any other personal relationship. The ego of the candidate often creates the greatest problem. How the candidate handles that ego is crucial to the success of the campaign. If he or she expects everyone working on the campaign to feed that ego, there is a problem.

(At this point, I ought to remark to the reader that it is obvious that I am writing from the perspective of a campaign chairman. Since much of my experience has been in that capacity, it is a natural vantage point from which to write. But I think you can read this as a candidate or worker and still find the points applicable.)

The candidate should not treat people on the campaign as employees unless they *are* in fact employees and receive a salary. Even so, when people are working for a salary on a campaign, they often are working for an amount considerably less than what they could receive in the private sector. So you cannot treat them as overpaid employees who will put up with all kinds of nonsense because they need to hang on to a fabulous salary. One of the basic facts of nearly all campaigns is that they pay as little as they can to get the job done, because resources are limited; sometimes this attitude is shortsighted. I mention it at this point because the candidate often sets the salary that will be paid.

Paid employees of a campaign should be treated with the same care that is afforded volunteers. This does not mean that paid staff members do not have to perform. Of course they do, and must be held accountable for the tasks assigned to them.

The confusion of reporting to both the candidate and the chairman can be handled by an agreement ahead of time that the campaign staff reports to the chairman and not directly to the candidate. This method proves difficult at times, because the chairman is seldom working on the campaign full time, and as a matter of expediting matters, the candidate may direct the campaign staff without bothering to inform the chairman. On more routine items, this may not cause problems, but the possibility exists that the staff may receive conflicting instructions. The campaign chairman may have directed the staff to spend the day recruiting volunteers for a particular section of the territory involved, and while doing this, the candidate may call and direct the staff to accompany him to a local shopping center for a day of campaigning. The problem is not which of these two campaign activities is more important; the problem is that the candidate is completely undercutting the authority and leadership of the chairman. In this situation, the candidate should telephone the chairman and tell him that he would like the staff to go with him to the local shopping center for the day. This gives the chairman and the candidate an opportunity to discuss the situation. If they agree, as is likely since the candidate still is the principal person in this drama, the chairman has the opportunity to explain the change to those involved.

This approach allows the chairman to maintain the proper relationship with the staff. If the candidate goes directly to the staff too often, the staff gets the idea that the chairman is just a figurehead. In some campaigns the chairman *is* a figurehead and the candidate is running the effort on his own. That is fine if everyone understands the situation. It's not when the chairman thinks he is chairing the effort, and the candidate considers him just a figurehead. There are not many chairmen of substance who will tolerate that situation for very long.

So whenever possible, the candidate should work through the chairman in the relationship with the staff and the volunteers.

It also is important that the candidate be even-tempered in dealing with people who are working on the campaign. It seldom is useful for the candidate to blow his cool or lose his temper. It may happen occasionally, but if it happens very often, it warrants a private conversation between the chairman and the candidate. It does not matter how important the matter is that causes the tantrum. The problem it creates is in the minds of the people working on the campaign. They may start having doubts as to how well qualified the candidate is to hold the office. This a valid concern. A campaign is solid training ground and can teach a potential office holder a great deal about the art of patience.

There are times when a candidate will be disappointed with something that is done or more likely something that is not done. Showing that disappointment or disapproval can be very effective at times, because nearly all of the people working want to please the candidate. But how the candidate expresses the disappointment is important.

It is essential that criticism, especially in meetings or groups, never be directed to an individual. It is the action or lack of it that should be criticized, never the person.

Let's take a couple of statements and see how a volunteer is likely to react to them.

Statement 1. Mary, you know I didn't want those signs on Elm Street. How did you screw up so badly?

Statement 2. We must have had some misunderstanding Mary. The signs were supposed to go up on College Avenue. How can we get them switched from Elm to College Avenue?

In both statements it is obvious that the signs are on the wrong street. In my opinion, Mary will go out of the meeting with her feelings hurt after hearing Statement 1. The campaign may lose her as a productive member of the team. She may get this particular situation corrected, but there is a good chance that for the rest of the campaign she will just go through the motions. She may quit.

With Statement 2, she has been given a face-saving device in that there may have been a misunderstanding. She was not attacked personally. She will get the correction taken care of and she will be retained for the campaign.

Many very dedicated campaign workers are lost because of the way mistakes are handled. The attitude is, "When I find out who screwed this up, heads will roll." Heads may roll, and the workers will roll right out of the campaign.

People on a campaign are most sensitive to the remarks of the candidate since he is the object of all the effort. If someone has to play the "heavy" in dealing with workers or volunteers, it is best that it be someone other than the candidate. If a volunteer gets upset with the candidate, the vote of that volunteer and all members of the family may be lost. If the volunteer, on the other hand, becomes unhappy with the campaign chairman, he may still believe that the candidate is "Mr. Wonderful." The volunteer may never vote for the campaign chairman, but then he is not the candidate. A campaign chairman must be sensitive to that kind of situation and help retain votes for the candidate. It is better to have the volunteer believe "the chairman is unreasonable but Joe's still my candidate," than "the candidate is insensitive to people and he is lucky to have such a wonderful person as chairman." The candidate and the chairman have to be sensitive to the ripple effect of such actions, and keep in mind that the idea of the whole effort is to collect votes, not to waste them.

This same philosophy applies to suppliers and other people who may do business with the campaign. Always maintain the position that retains or gains votes for the candidate. If someone has to get into delicate negotiations over a dubious bill where there are likely to be hard feelings, it shouldn't be the candidate.

Let's say the campaign is overcharged for a printing job and it is obvious that something has to be done. The candidate should not get involved in the negotiations. The chairman or the treasurer should do it so that the printer does not get upset with the candidate. After it is settled, the candidate should wait a day or two for cool heads to return (if it was that disagreeable) and then he should phone the printer or write a personally signed note.

Dear Joe,

I understand that there was a dispute with my campaign staff and your office about a printing bill.

It has been reported to me that the matter is now settled, thanks in large measure to your cooperative spirit. I trust it was settled to the satisfaction of all parties.

I just wanted to express my thanks to you for your assistance in bringing this matter to a successful conclusion.

Kindest personal regards,

Fred

Joe may think that the campaign staff is made up of a bunch of idiots, but there is a good chance that he thinks kindly of candidate Fred. Joe may influence ten or fifteen votes positively or negatively among members of his own family and circle of friends. Enough votes may be lost because of stands a candidate takes on divisive issues — there is no sense in losing votes over a printing bill. It is possible to refuse to be a patsy for people who may try to take financial advantage of political campaigns, but still not lose their votes.

Votes may be lost because a voter feels that the candidate ignored him at a political appearance. They are lost for many reasons that have absolutely nothing to do with the kind of office holder the individual would be. (I still feel that Tom Dewey lost a great deal of votes in 1948 because of a mustache which was not in vogue at that time. It was too close to World War II with Hitler's mustache, and about that time we were having a great deal of trouble with another famous mustache from Moscow on the face of Josef Stalin.) By being sensitive to the possibilities that exist in everyday situations for gaining or losing votes a candidate can make a difference in a close campaign.

Let's face it — many local elections are not decided over issues at all. They are popularity contests. When people feel deeply about an issue, they may vote for a candidate that they do not care for because of his or her position on an issue. The abortion issue is a good example of this kind of situation. But if there are no real issues, they will never vote for a candidate they do not like. This is why some candidates try to avoid a hot issue in order to be well-liked. If it is a very controversial topic they may alienate both sides. However, some are successful in avoiding the divisive issues.

As you can see, this relationship of the candidate to the organization reaches out beyond the campaign committee and the volunteers. It can touch a great cross section of the community.

In dealings with the campaign committee and the volunteers, the candidate should conduct himself as though his actions will become a matter of public information—because there is always a good chance that they will.

It is obvious that the candidate will like some people working on the campaign better than others. That is a natural human condition, but the candidate must not play favorites or real problems will be created. For example, if the candidate wants someone three levels down in the organization to be involved in strategy sessions, some corrective action needs to be taken. Either that person should be moved up in the organization where attendance at strategy meetings is a part of his new duties or other people three levels down should be encouraged to become involved in some strategy sessions. Personal jealousies can be very destructive and need to be recognized immediately. The best person to guard against such situations is the chairman or the executive director.

This brings up the subject of the kinds of titles that should be given to people in a campaign. As far as I am concerned, "captain" is the lowest title that should ever be assigned—there are no workers, corporals, or privates.

The person in charge of the campaign can be called the chairman or the campaign manager. Any title that is reasonably descriptive of the responsibilities that go with the job is suitable. A full-time paid person reporting to the chairman can be called the executive director, campaign manager (if the primary job is called chairman), or campaign coordinator. The secretary in the campaign office can be called executive secretary, campaign secretary, or campaign assistant. Treasurer is such an accurate title there does not appear to be a better one. A campaign can also have a budget director. In most cases this will be the treasurer's responsibility, but in a large campaign a separate individual might perform this function.

The individual who is in charge of fund raising can be called finance chairman, chief fund raiser, or resource chairman. The people responsible for a congressional district or legislative district could be called district chairmen. A person in charge of a ward could be called ward chairman. As a matter of fact, a chairman can exist at almost any geographic level. A campaign could even have a precinct chairman (but I prefer precinct captain), and if it gets down to each block, block captains can be assigned.

In some campaigns different titles are used at each level in the organization. This is not necessary and a lot of time is wasted devising titles. I would never use terms like "block worker" or "precinct volunteer." It is better to use a title that indicates the person is *in charge* of an area—he feels more responsible. You feel responsible for something you are in charge of—you do not feel that way if you are the "block worker."

These volunteers working on the campaign are not being paid, so the least you can do is give them some psychological pay with a title and some prestige.

Part II

The Campaign Plan and Strategy

8

The Image of Success

THIS STATEMENT HAS BEEN MADE about almost every business or endeavor: "If you're going to be successful, look successful." It applies to political campaigns equally as well.

A political campaign is to a large extent a matter of image. Unfortunately, many candidates are all image with no substance. Those are the kind of candidates who make poor office holders.

It is obvious that if your campaign is a shambles and the candidate looks like a loser, he is probably going to lose unless the opposition appears to be an even bigger loser. This is not as far-fetched as it sounds. How many times have you heard people say, "I don't like either one of them, so I guess I'll vote for the lesser of the two evils"? That is a situation where both candidates and campaigns have bad images.

It is possible for the candidate to come across positively in personal appearances but in other campaign efforts to project a negative impact. When this happens, the sheer magnetism of the candidate has to overcome all the negative vibrations. That is often too big a load to carry. Perhaps I can use a sports analogy to illustrate the point. Let's say you have a basketball team that has three outstanding players, but two who are below average. The three may be strong enough to overcome the negative influence of the other two, but your team would be in a stronger position against tough opponents if your entire team were strong. You can end up in a game that is so close that the three stars cannot overcome the drag caused by the other two. The absolute minimum you must expect from the two is that they be a neutral impact and not a negative one.

So it is in a campaign. Some parts of an effort may be neutral in their impact, but other segments are very positive. The answer is to emphasize the positives and work at creating the image of success.

This image of success has a two-fold purpose. Its primary purpose is to convince the voters to select the candidate. Its secondary purpose is to affect the opposition. If a candidate can get his opponent to believe that his campaign looks successful, it can have a direct impact upon his opponent's ability to recruit volunteers and raise money. These various reasons for having an image of success can be summed up with one statement: "It helps you win." And that is what it is all about.

Frankly, I have never believed in working in a campaign in which the goal was not to win. Strange as it may seem, there are candidates who are not in the race for the purpose of being elected. Let's talk about some of these people, primarily to help identify some of them if they happen to be opposing you.

There is the young attorney who gets into the race for the sole purpose of building up his law practice. Every time the campaign is covered in the news media, he is referred to as David Johnson, a Central City attorney who is a candidate for county commissioner. Now our friend David might not mind being a county commissioner, but perhaps he feels that some rather limited campaigning helps his community image, which does not hurt his law practice. I call this kind of campaigning an indirect form of professional advertising. We see a lot of this with young attorneys running for political office — they view it as a "no lose" situation.

Other candidates run for the sole purpose of articulating a particular point of view on one issue. They are deeply committed to a position and use the candidacy to bring attention to that issue. These candidates seldom win, but they often will determine who does win, as they siphon off enough votes from the major candidates to skew the outcome. These candidates can be very difficult to deal with, especially in joint appearances, because they have an emotional, religious fervor toward their position and logical, calm discussion of the issue is often impossible.

Then there are those candidates who are "doing it for a lark," just for the fun of it, and perhaps to make the so-called establishment uncomfortable. Sometimes, these candidates will take positions that shock nearly everybody except the small group of people who share their unusual beliefs on some of the issues. These are not always candidates of the extreme left — sometimes they are candidates of the extreme right also. These people seldom win elections, but they are a terrible nuisance to the candidates who do have a chance to win.

It is important to treat these candidates with respect. "Putting them down" won't necessarily gain them votes, but it may lose some for your own candidacy. People who may never have considered voting for these extreme-position candidates may judge you by your response to these candidates. The candidate who becomes the office holder will have to deal, at times, with individuals who may be just as much of an irritant.

Even if these candidates are considered a joke by nearly everyone, your public attitude toward them must be exemplary. You must at least act like you take them seriously.

A good rule to follow in political campaigning is never put anyone down. It seldom works to your benefit. You can disagree with your opponent. You can point out where he is wrong on a position. You can even state that he may not be qualified for the office. But do not ever humiliate him, because it can lose you votes. He may deserve to be put down or humiliated, but people may react strangely to your criticism. People may think he deserves it, but the minute you do it, they may feel sympathy for the "poor fellow."

Frankly, I think that if a candidate is going to put down the opposition, he has to do it in such a subtle way that he does not bring about this sympathy. It must be so subtle that the opponent does not realize it until he's on his way home from the joint appearance.

A good example of the not-so-subtle approach is the way Senator Dole went after Senator Mondale in the televised debate of the 1978 vice-presidential candidates. If Dole scored points for the number of times he went after Mondale's jugular, the debate would have been awarded to Dole. However everyone I know who saw the debate felt that Dole gained votes for the Carter-Mondale team. How a candidate conducts himself with the opposition, especially in joint appearances, is critical to the success of his campaign.

A candidate should always look successful. This means no extremes in dress unless that is the way his constituency dresses. Even the most liberal candidate in the world has better chances for success if he dresses "middle of the road." This also means no extreme hair styles.

If a candidate has young people campaigning for him, his image will be at stake. They do not have to dress in suits. (If they do, people will think they are from the Watchtower Society and would not answer the door.) They do not have to have short haircuts. But they do have to be neat and clean. This means hair is combed and clothes are clean. If someone is working on a campaign who insists on dirty, scraggly hair, dirty beard, and filthy clothes, he will have to work in the back room out of public view. A candidate does not need to worry about losing the dirty, scraggly vote — the dirty, scraggly constituency usually is not self-disciplined enough to register to vote.

If a candidate is female and attractive, that is fine. But she should not look sexy. That may be a desirable image, but not for getting elected. People do not want sexy office holders. That may be unfair, but a candidate for office who is an attractive female should not wear styles from Frederick's of Hollywood while in public unless she wants to lose. She should wear the kind of tailored business clothes she would wear in an office.

I am not going to get into the specifics of clothing and styles because styles change quickly, but I believe some of these general points will be helpful. Unfortunately, there are still many voters in this country who do not believe women have the temperament or the experience to be elected to office. It does not do any good to remind them of their prejudice—that just drives them deeper into it. However, I think a woman candidate who dresses in middle-of-the-road clothing and who is "cool" at all times can overcome some of these prejudices and be elected. The chances appear to be getting better each year.

This image of success is primarily a matter of attitude. Can you remember a day in your life when you really felt on top of the world? Perhaps it was a day when you accomplished a lifelong dream. Perhaps it was the day your child was born. Perhaps it was the day you received a promotion at work and a big raise. Perhaps it was the day you graduated from college. Pick a day in your life when you felt on top of the world; now translate that feeling into an attitude you can carry with you while out meeting people on the campaign trail. That kind of positive warmth transmits itself to people and is contagious.

When a candidate is visiting with people in a one-on-one situation, he should shake their hands firmly. A surprising number of voters complain that candidates are "like shaking hands with a dead fish."

When talking with voters while campaigning, a candidate should look them in the eye, but should not hold the look too long, especially with the opposite sex. For some reason, in this country a long look into the eyes of a member of the opposite sex has a sexual connotation and makes people uncomfortable. A candidate should look people in the eye, but should not hold the glance to the point they become uncomfortable.

Another way for a candidate to transmit a positive image is to carry himself as though he is already the office holder. This image will make people think, "That person looks like a commissioner." Another of my rules: "People seldom elect candidates that they believe will look uncomfortable in the job."

When arriving at a campaign appearance with a large attendance, a candidate should never go in alone if he or she can be accompanied by three or four campaign workers. A candidate walking into a crowded room of potential voters looks "lonesome," but one who comes in with three or four people as "friends" creates a better appearance. Another advantage is that the three or four people are available to pass out campaign material at the appropriate time. When making joint appearances with other candidates, he or she should assume that at least portions of the program will be recorded for radio or television news. This does a couple of things: our candidate will be prepared and will be dressed as he or she would want to be seen on a TV newscast.

Unfortunately the moderators at such events often are inexperienced at handling multiple-candidate appearances and are ignorant of the issues of the campaign. Therefore it becomes important for a candidate to come prepared with some statements to make when his turn comes to participate. He may take ten seconds to answer an irrelevant question and still find he has several minutes to speak. As he improves in public speaking he will learn how to make this transition.

Many qualified candidates for public office have lost political campaigns because they are inadequate public speakers. Often they are better qualified, but lose to someone who is better on his feet. You can be the most qualified candidate in the area, but if you are a poor public speaker you are at a real disadvantage.

As a candidate you do not have to be a spellbinder to get the job done. If you hate the thought of giving a speech, and if you cannot visualize yourself ever getting proficient and comfortable, then you should seriously reconsider running for public office. There are very few public offices that do not require the office holder to communicate to people in groups. If the thought of standing in front of a crowd of people and expressing your thoughts terrifies you, you can do one of two things: you can toss aside your ambitions to run for public office or you can do something about it.

I have a theory that one reason so many attorneys run for public office is that they already have this public speaking training — and they love the sound of their own voices. Maybe these traits helped them to pick their profession.

These arguments also apply to a campaign chairman. Occasionally two events are scheduled for the same time, and they both might be important enough that the campaign needs to be represented at both. A campaign chairman who cannot lead a group in silent prayer is of little help in this situation.

Fortunately, most people who find the idea of public speaking distasteful seldom think seriously of running for public office. But there still are many candidates who run for office who are poor speakers and need some help. The time to get this help is before they start running for office.

You can often find a course in public speaking at a local community college or an adult education program of the public school system. A college course in debating is also fine training for a candidate. Other ways to get such training are the Dale Carnegie Course and Toastmasters International. I am more familiar with Toastmasters, so I will elaborate on that.

Toastmasters is a nonprofit educational organization whose members share the common goal of improving their listening, thinking, and speaking skills. There are no professional instructors in Toastmasters. These are amateurs helping each other. Some individuals may be fairly new while others are very proficient speakers who remain in the club because they enjoy it or they consider the ninety minutes each week as the insurance premium they pay to stay sharp in the art of public speaking.

The magic ingredient, I believe, that makes Toastmasters so workable and effective is the set of professional manuals made available to the members for their modest dues. Anyone who goes through the three Toastmaster manuals has the opportunity to become an accomplished speaker. You can improve your skills tremendously by going through only the first manual.

This kind of training is valuable to any candidate. You and I have both heard candidates for the highest offices in the land who could have been more effective in communicating if they had had some public speaking training.

Unfortunately many candidates, and perhaps the reader, believe that it is their approach to the issues and their great devotion and integrity that warrant their being elected. But if you are not at least an adequate public speaker, you are subtracting points from your chance of being elected. If you cannot communicate your approach to the issues, and if your great devotion and integrity does not come shining through in your ability to speak both formally and informally, you are not maximizing your opportunities to get elected.

Another part of the Toastmaster program that is invaluable to a would-be politician is its ability to improve extemporaneous speaking skills. Called "Table Topics" in Toastmasters, it is intended to improve your ability to think on your feet. This is a skill that is especially valuable to a candidate. Here is how it works:

One of the members will be assigned the duty of "Topic Master" for a night. It is his responsibility to devise a list of subjects and call upon people to speak on one of them for approximately two minutes. The Topic Master will usually call only on those members who are not assigned a formal speech for that evening.

The Topic Master will usually read the subject aloud and

then call on a member. The time the speaker has to think about what he will say is the time it takes to walk to the lectern from his chair. It is sometimes frightening for the newer members, but since everyone else has experienced the same feelings, the speaker is addressing an empathetic audience.

It will not take the would-be politician long to realize what excellent training this is for handling reporters' questions or questions from an audience at campaign appearances. It is important that a candidate be able to answer questions as effectively as possible. He cannot be effective if he has butterflies in his stomach, shaky knees, and cotton in the mouth. The place for these is at the Toastmaster meeting where they will be treated with kindness and understanding, not on the campaign trail where his discomfort will be translated into loss of votes.

If you and your opponent are relatively equal in qualifications for the office, but you can handle yourself on your feet and he or she cannot, your chances to win are greatly increased. The more joint appearances you make, the better for your candidacy.

I have known of candidates whose opponents were such poor public speakers that they worked at drumming up organizations to sponsor joint appearances — every time they would appear together the good speaker would gain votes and the poor speaker would lose votes. The reader may think this is unfair — the poor speaker might actually be a better office holder than the good speaker. I am not talking about what is fair and what should be — I am talking about the way it is.

The time to develop these skills as a public speaker is *before* you run for office. You cannot develop these skills *while* you are running for office. If you do, you run the risk of losing some votes before your skills are sharpened.

Do not take the approach, "If I run and lose, then before I run again, I will develop the speaking skills." The trouble with that approach is that you are going into the campaign with an unnecessary liability. Also, people who receive a negative impression of your candidacy the first time you run may not see you in person the second time you run, and will vote against you because of their recollection of your first campaign.

Obviously, if you have already lost a campaign you cannot go back and change anything, so by all means develop the speaking skills before you run again.

Do not think you can develop the necessary skills by buying a book on speaking. Unless you go out and practice those skills, the chance of improving is pretty remote. It is like reading a great instruction book on golf for a week before the club tournament comes up — without practice, reading that book won't translate into improved scoring.

Stop and think of how much time a candidate spends in communicating to the electorate. It does not make much sense for him to be a poor communicator. But I am constantly amazed at the number of candidates who are just that.

Have you ever noticed how some people when speaking connect phrases together with an "ah"? They do this as a time-buying device. They are using time to think or to solidify in their own minds what they are going to say. There is one major problem with this habit and it is — that it's a bad habit. If a speaker does it a lot, it makes him sound indecisive to an audience. The more he does it, the more unsure of himself he sounds. That loses votes.

Two words that some people use in place of "ah" are "you know." They are used everywhere and anywhere. The constant repetition of this phrase makes a speaker's vocabulary sound extremely limited.

Both of these speech habits should be avoided. Almost everyone develops speaking phrases that they fall in love with and keep using over and over. There is nothing wrong with using them if it is done sparingly. They should not be repeated over and over because they detract from the image of success.

These phrases or connectors are used almost subconsciously and you may not be aware that you use them as often as you do. It is a great training device to have your early political speeches tape-recorded so that you can hear what you sound like. The first time to do this is in front of a group of your dedicated supporters. They will be a very friendly audience. There is nothing wrong with giving your first speeches of the campaign in front of your supporters. It will build up your confidence and it is certainly an audience that you can relax with. You can even have them throw questions to you at the end of your talk, and the tougher the better.

If you are like most people, you will be more critical of yourself than anyone else. And your supporters will try to convince you that you do not sound as bad as you think you do.

Another real asset to campaigning is a video tape recorder. This gives you an opportunity to see yourself as others see you. It may be a very sobering experience, but you are your own toughest audience.

When you get into a real campaign appearance, have it taped and listen to it critically with other members of your campaign committee. If you tape your speeches, and debates, and questions and answers that are thrown at you, you will be amazed at how much you improve from your very first efforts compared to your speeches toward the end of the campaign.

In joint appearances, too many candidates look at each other when they are answering questions. Do not look at the other candidates or the moderator. The other candidates are certainly not going to vote for you and the moderator is also questionable. Look at your audience. Those voters in your audience are the ones you want to convince.

Should You Hire an Agency?

The hiring of an agency involves the whole area of image. The decision to do so will depend on whether or not you can afford it.

If you cannot afford it, try to have someone on your campaign committee or staff with at least some journalism background to help with publicity.

There are two things that nearly everyone believes they're expert in — public relations and politics. Combine these two and you have the potential for bad advice, bad information, and bad decisions.

There are several advantages that an advertising agency can bring to your campaign. Agency people work daily with concepts of image. They make their living by presenting a product in the most favorable light that they can develop. They work regularly with film and sound. You cannot, in my opinion, use television or radio ads without professional assistance. You are running some real risks if you attempt a do-it-yourself approach. Television especially is so expensive that you cannot afford to spend that kind of money without professional help. Media people work regularly in putting images on film; they know who the good film crews are, and who the outstanding film editors are.

Selecting an agency is not easy. You will probably talk to several. It's advantageous if you can select one that has handled some successful political campaigns. That is a proven track record and can be reassuring. However just because an ad agency worked on a losing campaign does not mean that its workers are not a talented group of people.

Do not eliminate an ad agency just because its staff has never worked a political campaign. Everybody has to have a first time. The fact that they have not worked on an election before does not mean that they are lacking in creative ability. It may be that they are not jaded with a lot of preconceived notions and you could receive some fresh ideas. While I prefer an agency with some political experience, I do not think you should automatically eliminate those who would be working their first political campaign.

You cannot call an ad agency and say "send me a proposal." You have to spend some time discussing your campaign, so the agency people can get a feel for what you are trying to accomplish. Every agency that you are considering should be requested to submit to you a written proposal, based on the media budget you quote. Rates should be similar from one to another. You should not make the decision based solely on the dollars to be expended, but on the ideas that are proposed.

In most cities that have several ad agencies, you can usually find out which agencies handle which campaigns. There are some agencies that handle only Democratic candidates and some that handle only Republicans. Some may handle either political party. For nonpartisan elections, you may just have to find out what is available. Ask people who have been around campaigns for some length of time about the situation in your community. If you are a conservative Republican, there is no sense wasting your time talking to an agency that only handles Democratic candidates, and vice versa.

You are not restricted to agencies in your own community or even your own state. If you are running for a state-wide office, you have a greater number of agencies to choose from. If you are running for a city office, there is some advantage to using a local ad agency. The staff knows what is going on in the community — it does not have to learn the unusual facets of the campaign or the locale. However, do not use a local agency for the sake of using a local agency if you are convinced through your research that it cannot do a satisfactory job for you. It is a fair credo to "spend your campaign money locally," but it is foolish to throw it away. If you have to go out of town or out of state to get a satisfactory agency, that is preferable to using a local one that does inferior work. Recognize, however, that you may be criticized for not using hometown people.

If you are involved in a campaign for the first time, you need to talk to more than one agency so that a fair comparison can be made. The most important factor is how you react to the people you are going to be working with. This is most significant for the candidate and the chairman, because if there is not a good relationship, it will be a problem throughout the entire campaign. There is no sense in hiring an agency if these two key people have any misgivings about it.

As I have stated earlier, most candidates are rather strong

people who have set ideas about what they believe and what they want. However, a candidate hires an ad agency because its staff members are experts in their field; therefore he should listen when they speak about the use of their skills to help in his campaign. If the candidate and the chairman are going to provide *all* of the ideas, then they do not need an ad agency, all they need are messengers.

There are ad agencies, I am sure, that will accept all your ideas, even the bad ones, because they want the income. But be willing to listen to their creative ideas. When you combine your ideas about the campaign and your thoughts about the issues with a creative ad agency's expert advice, you then will be getting what you are paying for.

Of course there are incompetent ad agencies. There are also agencies that do a great job of selling potato chips but will do a bad job of packaging a candidate. That is why you should not make a hasty selection.

You need to develop a completely open and frank relationship with your agency. If you think its approach is "too slick" or uncomfortable for you, then you must say so. You have to be comfortable with its proposals about your campaign. The fact is that many times, an advertising agency makes a candidate look like the "second coming" and the candidate does not object. You seldom complain if someone makes you look better than you really are, but you can become irate if you are made to look worse than you think you are.

It is beyond the scope of this book to attempt to tell you what kind of an ad campaign you ought to run. That is going to vary by what kind of a race you are in, how big the territory is, and how much money you have to spend.

When considering an ad agency, do not deal exclusively with the president of the firm; get acquainted with the other people who work there. The quality of the agency's work depends on the quality of its people.

It is not unusual for small ad agencies to be primarily one-man operations, even though a number of people work there. In such situations all major decisions are made by the head of the firm — all creative ideas come from that person, and everyone who works there merely carries out his instructions. This may be all right if the president is a genius, but there are not many of those around. Another danger present when only one person generates the ideas and makes the decisions is that everything comes grinding to a halt if that individual goes on vacation, gets sick, or drops dead.

In most cases, you will be better off with an ad agency that has several bright, creative people on the staff. You will then have the assurance that the recommendations are the combined thinking of several people.

The charges from an ad agency should be discussed well in advance of your commitment. Do not go into an open-ended arrangement.

Some agencies will earn their primary income by charging a percentage of the cost of the media advertising placed, usually fifteen percent. Production costs are added on top of that. In other words, if you know how much you are going to spend on placing media, under normal circumstances the ad agency would receive fifteen percent of that. In addition there are the production costs of your TV ads, radio spots, brochures, and the printing of the material.

Another method that may be used is for the agency to keep track of the time spent working on the campaign and charge you by the hour. While the ad agency may prefer this type of open-ended arrangement, you must know what the limit of the expense will be. The ad agency does not have to raise the money to cover expenses — the campaign committee does.

9

The Budget

THERE ARE TWO BASIC APPROACHES to budgeting for a political campaign: One is to determine how much money you think it is going to take to conduct a successful campaign and then attempt to raise it; the other is to determine how much money you think you can raise, and then tailor your campaign to fit those financial restraints.

Very few campaigns have as much money as they would like to have. As a result most campaign committees follow both methods mentioned above. They start out by calculating how much money they think it will take, and then later they scale it down to what they can raise. Sometimes the candidate personally goes into debt. That has to be a decision made only by the candidate, but it is not one I can recommend at all. I have seen candidates lose close elections and then spend the next decade trying to get out of debt.

In nearly all jurisdictions where people run for political office, there are reporting requirements for campaigns. If you want to get an idea of how much was spent in previous campaigns for the office you seek, those financial reports are usually a matter of public record, and so you do have access to them. You can see how much money was raised, who contributed it, and how it was spent. It depends on the jurisdiction and the laws governing those campaign reports, but it may be possible for you to get copies of the reports. In some places, you are allowed to look at them, but not copy them.

If you look at the campaign reports of previous efforts, do not fall into the trap of drawing incorrect conclusions from the numbers you are looking at. You cannot assume that the losing candidate necessarily lost because of financial consider-ations. He could have lost because he was a terrible cam-paigner, or because the other candidate was perceived as being more qualified for the office.

What follows is a list of some typical expense items that could be a part of a campaign budget.

Ad agency expenses	Office supplies
Brochures	Polling expenses
Bumper stickers	Postage
Campaign pins	Rent for office space
Direct mail expense	Rental of equipment
Election night party expense	Staff salaries
F.I.C.A. taxes	Telegraph
Fund raising expenses	Telephone
Handout material	Travel expenses
Letterheads and envelopes	Unemployment taxes
Media	Yard signs
Miscellaneous	

Not all campaigns will have all of these expenses and some will have bills not listed here. Most of these expenses are self-explanatory or are discussed in other chapters of this book.

In preparing your budget, the income side will be rather lim-ited. The income comes almost exclusively from contribu-tions. It can also come from other fund-raising projects, but most of those will require your reporting the individual contri-butions. Other income might come from a loan by the candi-date to the campaign. Oftentimes that loan will come from a personal loan the candidate secures from his own bank. The regulations may vary, so if your campaign has a loan involved, be sure you know how to report it.

One reason many candidates report personal money to a campaign as a loan is because they are optimistic that enough money will be raised in order to repay the loan. If the candidate makes a large contribution and reports it as a contribution, it can hardly be repaid because no debt exists. This becomes important when you start looking like a winner, because people may jump on your bandwagon with contributions, and you can then be repaid. This is one reason you will often hear candidates say, "He was with me early." Being a supporter early when the outcome is questionable is more important than becoming a supporter once the bandwagon arrives. Candidates recognize the difference.

The budget preparation is usually a joint operation involving the chairman, treasurer, finance chairman, and the candidate. If there is a finance committee, its primary function will determine if it gets involved in the budget preparation. If the finance committee is assembled for the purpose of raising money, then it may not be involved in the preparation of the budget.

Along with the budget, those involved in the campaign need to know who is authorized to commit the expenditure of campaign funds. Unfortunately, people working on campaigns get carried away in the emotionalism of the contest and incur some expenses without thinking. Therefore everyone with a responsible position on the campaign needs to know the rules. A good rule to follow is that the office manager, executive director, or campaign coordinator can authorize the purchase of office supplies up to a certain limit. In a small-budget campaign this limit might be as low as twenty-five or fifty dollars. With a larger campaign, such as a congressional campaign, it might be $100 or $200.

One aspect of the financial planning beyond the budget preparation is a cash-flow projection. People involved in political campaigns do this either in their heads or more formally on paper. It is better to do it on paper, so that everyone knows the requirements.

A cash-flow projection merely estimates at what points various expenditures will be made. Here are some questions you might ask:

1. When must our newspaper ads be paid?

2. When must we pay for our radio and TV ads?

3. When should we print our brochures and when must we pay?

4. When will we mail our advertising? How much will that postage be?

To follow up on this concept, look over your entire budget and determine when expenses are going to hit; then you need to match those expenses with sufficient income to pay for them. The better you can do in anticipating the timing of expenses, the more accurate information you can provide to those people in the campaign who will raise the money. It is important that they realize *when* the campaign must have the money. For example, if thirty percent of your expenses will be incurred in the first sixty days, then the finance people need to have that income available by that time.

Many of the greatest frustrations in political campaigns come about because the expense projections are not matched with sufficient income. That is why it is so important to create a realistic budget; realistic can be defined as "the money that we are able to raise." If you raise more money than the budget calls for, it is a fairly simple matter to decide where to direct the additional revenue. The reverse is seldom true—trying to cut back on the budget to match reduced income is much more difficult.

No matter how well political campaigns are planned, the last few weeks are always hectic. Without solid budgetary planning they are chaotic.

10

Political Polling

MOST PEOPLE BELIEVE THAT POLITICAL polling is something that is done only by Gallup, Roper, or Lou Harris. A second impression they have is that polls are taken to find out who is going to win the election.

Sophisticated computerized polls can be taken involving "typical" precincts. At the other extreme are simple polls that a campaign committee can conduct to learn useful information for its own purposes. In between those two extremes are a variety of other polls.

Before you hire a pollster of your own, find out if the local newspaper, TV station, or radio station is going to conduct a poll. See if you can determine what questions will be asked and when the poll will be run. If the poll will be run early enough to do you any good, it may save you from running your own poll.

You could also approach the pollster and see if it is possible to add one or two questions to the poll which you would pay for. This arrangement would in all probability be checked back with the original contractors to make certain that they did not object to your piggybacking onto their poll. If they did not object, this approach would be much less expensive than doing an entire poll of your own.

Unfortunately, most of the polls taken by the media for their readers, viewers, or listeners are taken so close to the election that the information is received too late to properly react to it. A poll published the week before the election will not allow you any long-range planning. About all it can do is create a feeling of apathy in the candidate shown to be ahead, and cause the one who is behind to work harder the last few days.

If you cannot afford a pollster of your own, you may want to hire a pollster to at least design the questions for you. This would lessen the cost tremendously. However the pollster will not guarantee the accuracy of the results if you are using your volunteers to do the calling. Pollsters will not take the responsibility for people they do not control; this is a perfectly understandable position.

Elections are seldom a one-race affair, except in those states where the election laws provide for a run-off. Therefore in your race there are no doubt other campaigns going on at the same time. Some of the candidates may be friends of yours or political allies. It can be helpful to include some of these people in your poll and share the cost.

There are many advantages to using a professional pollster. Before hiring one, see what the company's track record has been for past elections. The staff will be happy to show you the statistics on the ones that they called right on target; finding out about ones they missed might be more difficult.

If you have the money to hire a professional pollster, the staff hired will need to know what information you are seeking. Before you hire a firm, check out its credentials. How long has it been in business? If it is new, was it previously a part of another reputable firm? The fact that it is a new firm should not exclude it from consideration if the proper background and experience exist.

You can probably get by with conducting your own poll in a medium-size community. Attempting to take a state-wide poll or a congressional district poll on your own can be difficult.

You can learn from newspaper polls previously taken in your community how many people need to be polled in order to get a representative sample of the voters.

Many candidates want to use a poll as an ego trip. They want to find out how popular they are rather than to obtain information that will help them win the election. What are you going to do with the information you get? If you find out that you are far behind, are you going to drop out of the race? If you find out you are way ahead, are you going to change what you are doing? Unless a poll is likely to give you information that you are going to act on, do not bother with all the work necessary to gather the sample. Some campaign committees go to a lot of work to gather information and then do not make use of it.

You can use a couple of approaches in taking your poll. You can poll the entire community by selecting names from each page in the local telephone book. To do this, pick a certain number — let's say ten — and then call the tenth name in the second column of each page. If the tenth name is a business, go to the first residential name following it.

Another way of polling is to research previous election results and see if there are one or two precincts that are typical of the entire community. In other words, are there precincts which are microcosms of the city? If they were right on the nose in past elections, you may want to poll those entire precincts to gather your information.

Professional pollsters have told me that they can ask twenty-five or thirty questions if they design the questions in such a way that the person being polled does not feel threatened by them. My own personal reaction is that if I am called by a poll, I start getting irritated after a few questions. It may be my political experience that makes me suspicious of polls.

If you are going to use your volunteers to do this polling, there are some rules that you must follow if the information is to be of any value.

1. Never identify your campaign committee. You are calling on behalf of "Community-wide Opinion Polling Associates" or "State Polling Associates" or some such name. If you identify that you are the "Smith for Council Committee" the information you receive is worthless. Those polled may be influenced by who they think is asking the questions. If people respond by asking, "Who are you taking this poll for?" your answer is, "I am sorry, we are not allowed to give out that information." At that point some people will tell you that they will not participate in the poll. When that happens, always be courteous, thank them, and terminate the call.

2. Tell people that their number was selected at random and no record will be kept of the numbers called. You are just interested in their opinion, and not in who gave the opinion. If they ask if you are keeping track of who you are calling, answer no, and mean it. Keep track of the information only.

3. Never ask the questions you are most interested in at the start of the poll. If people are uncomfortable with being polled, their answers to the first few questions are likely to be the most guarded and therefore not representative of their true feelings. The questions most significant to your campaign should be placed about eighth or ninth for two reasons. Those polled will usually be most relaxed by that time, if they ever relax; and it is early enough in the poll that they have not yet become tired of the questions. (I guess I am not typical of people called for polls, because I am very reluctant to answer questions of this type over the phone. I am amazed, however, at what people will tell you over the phone when you are conducting a poll.) The first few questions therefore should be questions that people are likely to answer. It is best to pick an issue that is well-known in your community and one on which nearly everyone will have an opinion. For example, if there is a bond issue, you might ask about that first. "Issue questions" seem to be more comfortable for people to handle than "candidate questions."

4. Never ask how people are going to vote *in a direct manner*. Never say, "If the election were held tomorrow, would you vote for Fred Smith or Ted Jones?" That kind of question invites the response, "None of your business." I believe it is better to ask, "If the election were held tomorrow would you be *inclined to* vote for Fred Smith or Ted Jones?" Perhaps the distinction is minor, but I believe the second question is more likely to receive a response. I know that some professional pollsters disagree with my point of view. You ought to solicit the advice of one you know if you are going to design your own questions.

5. Never argue with the person you are polling. If the person gets hostile, terminate the conversation quickly and diplomatically. It can be as brief as, "Thank you anyway, I am sorry to have disturbed you."

A poll can help you design the thrust of the campaign. It is true that some candidates do not actually make a public statement on an issue until they know the results of a poll. This is described as "finding out which way the parade is going and then jumping out front to appear to be leading it." Even presidential candidates have been known to use this approach. While it may be hypocritical for a candidate to take a position that is contrary to the way he actually feels, the purpose here is not to make moral judgments, but to discuss ways to win an election. In most situations, candidates with any integrity will not reverse their position on an issue because of what a poll shows. However they may deemphasize that issue. What is likely to happen is that a candidate who does not feel strongly about a certain issue may go ahead and support the side that the poll supports. There are such issues. In a city election, a zoning question may be a hot issue. If the candidate feels that he could support either position, and his polls show that seventy percent of the people are opposed to the zoning, which way do you think the candidate will go?

Some political science students consider such reaction to polls a sell-out on idealism. They believe that you ought to have deeply held political convictions about all issues and then go out with extraordinary eloquence and convince the entire constituency of your views. Democratic representative government seldom works that way. As the English novelist John Galsworthy said, "Idealism increases in direct proportion to one's distance from the problem."

11

Sizing Up
the Competition

IF YOU COULD GET INTO the minds of voters, you would find that most believe they will vote for the better-qualified candidate. A campaign provides the opportunity for a candidate to exploit his strengths and his opposition's weaknesses. That is what a campaign is for—you try to convince the voters that you are the more qualified of the candidates, or that you are likely to provide the type of office holder that they want.

Let us look at various approaches that might be used.

1. Qualified Candidate. I should not list this approach by itself because this is what all the other approaches are destined to accomplish. I mention it here primarily because its absence would appear to be an oversight.

2. Experience. The experience factor can be positive or negative. This approach is usually quite successful for the incumbent. The old cliché "Don't change horses in the middle of the stream" has been done so long and so often that it should be avoided. There are other ways of conveying the same idea. "You do not send in the freshman quarterback in a crucial situation when you have the experienced quarterback who has brought you to the bowl game."

Experience can work against a candidate if many unpopular

decisions have been made during his term of office. A candidate running against such an incumbent can point out that the kind of experience the office holder has had certainly has not been in the best interest of the voters, or that it does not reflect the viewpoints of the voters. This is one way to reverse the impact of experience.

Experience certainly is not limited to the office being sought. If an office seeker has held other offices, those can be listed in his advertising as qualifications for the job. Various civic activities and accomplishments can be mentioned. He should evaluate each civic activity very carefully before including it. Will that activity be considered a plus or a minus? He may not be in a position to fairly evaluate this as the candidate. Others associated with the campaign committee may be able to bring fresh evaluation to the question.

3. Fresh Insight, or the Common Sense Approach. This factor is tied in tightly with experience. It works best for a candidate who is running against an incumbent or for someone who is outside the stream of political thought that exists in the current body (such as city council or school board). The common sense approach is used often because it works; the reason it works is because people feel that if politicians "would just use a little common sense we would not have all the problems we have." It appeals to many voters because they believe they have common sense whether they do or not. People may agree more readily with Lincoln when he said, "God must have loved the common man because he made so many of them," than with writer Philip Wylie who complained, "God must have hated the common man because he made him so damn common."

This fresh insight or common sense approach is also used as related to government financing. It is usually contained in a statement about budgets, such as, "When Mrs. Smith and I sit down to work on the family budget and pay the bills, we cannot spend money that we do not have. We need to balance that budget and if there is not enough money, we have to decide what we will do without." Even U.S. Presidents have used that argument — it is still effective even though it may lack validity. Everybody is for cutting back spending as long as it does not slice the program they have an interest in. The fresh insight or common sense approach can still be effective, but if carried too far it may hint of demagogy.

I worked on a campaign in which the opponent carried the common sense approach too far. He had very simple solutions to every complex issue. We suggested that "one reason he appears to have all the answers is because he has not yet heard all of the questions." (Like many political lines, I do not know the origin of that statement. I am sure we thought it was original at the time.)

4. The Organization Candidate. You can often tell if a friend is going to seek political office by all the new organization affiliations he collects. This is done for a two-fold purpose; it looks good on ads and brochures, and it increases the chances that people in those organizations will vote for one of their own. This approach can backfire. Members of an organization might rightly resent being used by a candidate. So if a candidate is going to use this approach, it cannot be blatant. It works best if it is not used as a campaign maneuver but is coincidental. If he already belongs to a lot of organizations it may be effective to point out these organizations in his material. It is obvious, however, that if he is in a geographic area that is seventy-five percent Roman Catholic (or whatever) and he is a member of St. Anthony's parish, it would be a mistake *not* to mention it in his campaign material.

It is my opinion that a long list of organizations can be counter-productive. A reasonable number (eight to ten) might be helpful.

5. Endorsements. There are two kinds of endorsements. One is the endorsement of a well-known political figure. The campaign staff has to decide whether such an endorsement would be helpful to their effort. An endorsement from an outside political figure could work against a campaign. The oppo-

sition could say that "we do not need outsiders to tell us how to vote." If the political figure doing the endorsing is registered to vote in the election, that objection has been overcome.

The other type of endorsement involves long lists of people in ads or brochures who support the candidate. Again, a judgment must be made as to whether or not this will help the campaign. One theory is that voters reading the ad or brochure will be impressed with the people who are endorsing, either because it is a long impressive list or because of the prominence of the names listed. The other theory is that if there is one name on the list that turns the voter off, that negative image will be transferred to the candidate.

Using the endorsement approach can be very effective and help create a bandwagon impression — but there is some danger to it.

This brings us to that delicate subject of how to point out the faults of your opponent without looking like a mudslinger yourself. I believe that there are certain lines you do not cross in a political campaign. If your opponent has a serious drinking problem to the point that he is an active alcoholic, it is obvious that he can't do the job in the office he seeks. But you cannot run ads referring to yourself as "the sober candidate for council," as much as you might like to. Rather than get involved with such charges yourself, it would be better to have a third party not connected with either campaign to look into the matter. This is the kind of situation where discreet inquiries might be made to an investigative reporter from an objective newspaper; the campaign chairman might talk to a reporter that he or she trusts.

If the opponent does not have a drinking problem, the reporter's investigation ought to show that. If there is a problem, that newspaper has a tough editorial decision to make. You have discharged your responsibility by bringing it to someone who is trained to objectively dig out facts. I do not believe that a campaign officer or the candidate should take it any further.

There are some situations that develop in a campaign where the shortcomings of your opponent are a legitimate issue in the race. If you and your opponent are seeking the office of treasurer of some political subdivision, and your opponent has declared bankruptcy and is a deadbeat about paying his bills, that is a legitimate concern and one that the voters have a right to know about. The way you bring this up is important.

Many times the "protected source" of a reporter is the opposition candidate who has much to gain from the information becoming public. I see nothing wrong with feeding these kinds of inquiries to a reporter, as long as the reporter and his newspaper or broadcasting station have integrity.

If you go after the bankrupt candidate publicly, you are liable to be accused of dirty politics and you might evoke sympathy for him. However, if you are in a face-to-face confrontation with your opponent and he is hitting hard at his qualifications, you will have to decide whether or not you bring it up. How you say it is important. I think in such situations you must always be the master of the understatement.

Do not say, "You are not qualified because you are a deadbeat who's cheated all his creditors by claiming bankruptcy." Do not say it even if it is true. If you must say it, this way is better: "We all recognize that many people run into financial difficulties from time to time. Everyone can identify with that and be sympathetic to that situation. However, when we are talking about handling the public's money in the office of treasurer, then the financial integrity of the candidate does become a concern. There should rightfully be a question in the mind of voters as to whether a person recently bankrupt should make financial decisions about public money." I think the second statement is the more correct and humane way to approach the issue.

There are other situations that can be handled in a similar manner. People are perceptive enough nowadays so that the old political maneuvers no longer can be foisted upon a gullible public. As an example, let's assume that one of the candidates is elderly and it is questionable whether he is physically strong enough to serve. His opponent might constantly say, "As far as I am concerned, my opponent's age is not an issue in this campaign." By saying it is not an issue, he constantly reminds people of his opponent's age. I do not believe the voters buy that kind of hypocrisy anymore.

There are other ways of exploiting your own strengths and your opponent's weaknesses. I make no judgment as to whether they are proper techniques for your campaign.

If your opponent is young and inexperienced, your campaign material can refer to you as mature and experienced.

If your opponent is elderly and fragile, you can be referred to as vigorous and capable of doing the job.

If your opponent is an incumbent with a lot of experience you can be full of new vision, fresh ideas, and concepts.

You can state your qualifications for the job in a positive way and still draw the distinctions between yourself and your opponent.

As previously mentioned, if your opponent is a terrible speaker, you want to draw him into as many joint appearances as possible. There are always organizations that are willing to sponsor such "debates." If you are confident you will look good and make the opponent look bad, you could consider having the debate video-taped. You could rightfully get into difficulty if you edited it for TV ads, but if you bought the time and showed the entire debate no one could criticize that approach to give the viewing audience an opportunity to see both candidates.

Voters get very weary of candidates who only talk about the incompetency of their opponents. People do not buy this kind of completely negative campaigning anymore. So while you can refer to your opponent and the areas of his or her shortcomings, you have to run your own campaign. Instead of talking constantly about your opponents, you must put forth some positive vibrations. You have to talk about what you are going to do if you are elected to the office. You need to tell people why they should vote for you. You cannot conduct an entire campaign based on the reasons why your opponent should not be elected.

Many a candidate has been elected by virtually ignoring the opposition. While I do not necessarily recommend it, it does indicate that you do not have to spend all your time knocking the opposition in order to win. That is often counter-productive.

Sometimes groups interested in a single issue will get involved in a campaign because of their position on that issue. If you happen to be on their side of the issue, such a group may not only make financial contributions, but also run ads or support your candidacy with their membership. You have to consider again whether or not such a group helps or hurts you. Sometimes such groups are not so much for you as they are against your opponent. If they want to help your campaign they ought to consult with you about how they can be most effective. Unfortunately many one-issue groups are so emotionally involved in their cause that they consult absolutely no one.

This entire matter of drawing distinctions between the opponent and yourself requires a proper balance—in fact, it should weigh heavier toward the positive aspects of your own campaign. If you dwell too much on the negative aspects of your opponents, what will you do if you are involved in a primary election campaign with seven or eight other candidates? You cannot spend all of your effort pointing out how rotten they all are. While it may come as a shock to you, there is a chance that some of them may be as qualified as you are. So you must get on with your own campaign and not spend an inordinate amount of time wallowing in the middle of an opponent's campaign.

12

Issues—Which Ones and How Many?

AFTER A CANDIDATE DECIDES TO run, he or she then wants to become knowledgeable about the issues. Many times it is a deep concern about the issues involved that triggers the decision to become a candidate.

The candidate obviously has to know something about the office being sought before making a decision to pursue it. Perhaps it is better stated to say that the candidate *should* know something about the office.

It is not always a deep commitment to an issue that causes an individual to seek an office. A person may choose to run for the office that he thinks he has the best chance of winning. This is brought about by an assessment of the existing political situation.

A person might feel that he'd like to run for county clerk, but it would mean upsetting a popular incumbent in the primary election. However, the county treasurer is retiring and therefore the office is more likely to be won. This kind of reasoning goes on all the time—it often is not the desire for a particular office, but the desire to hold *some* office that encourages a candidate to run.

Some people get their kicks from being candidates. They enjoy the running and all the attention that comes from being an office seeker. Some of these people get bored with the office itself and will often run for another office in the middle of their term. They need the attention a campaign brings.

What does all this have to do with the issues? It may mean that the candidate knows very little about the issues, and must learn about the issues and master them before the heat of the campaign.

In an election in which the candidate may have to face a multitude of issues, it is a good idea to put together an issue and research committee composed of people who know or can learn rather quickly what the issues are. It is obvious that a candidate for governor or Congress is going to have more issues to face than is a candidate for clerk of the district court. The candidate or the campaign chairman needs to decide rather soon after the decision is made to run whether or not an issue and research committee is needed.

If you do appoint such a committee, select one of the members to be its chairman so that the group does not waste time. People selected for the issue and research committee should already have knowledge of some of the issues. These may be people who come in contact with the office with some degree of regularity and know what the problems are. The main qualification for a member of the issue and research committee is the ability to look at questions with some objectivity and then make recommendations to the campaign committee and the candidate. It helps if this individual has good political instincts too, so that he can perceive how voters are likely to react to certain positions.

The committee should put no limit on the number of issues they study. They should study all the issues important to the office and the campaign. They should recommend a position to the candidate on each of those issues.

They should then narrow the issues down to two groups of three issues each. One group should be made up of those three issues that the committee believes are the most important. The other group should be composed of those three issues that they believe the candidate should emphasize in his or her campaign. The two groups may overlap. (This information may tie in closely with the information gathered from a poll, if a poll is conducted.)

The candidate should become intimately acquainted with every issue that the committee studies. If the candidate disagrees with any of the recommendations of the committee, he should discuss these differences with the committee. The committee members should understand from the beginning that not all of their recommendations will be accepted. They may suggest positions that the candidate simply disagrees with or feels are politically unsound positions for him to take.

All of the issues should be studied by the candidate because they may come up for discussion during the course of the campaign.

Of the two groups of three issues that the committee recommends as "most important" and "should be emphasized," the candidate and his campaign committee will need to decide which three issues will be accentuated during the campaign.

Why three? Some campaigns may involve hundreds of issues. If a candidate for any office speaks about all of the issues that may exist, that candidate's public identity will become lost. The reaction is likely to be, "Here's a candidate who knows something about everything but feels deeply about nothing."

A good rule to follow is this: Pick three issues that you believe (with some agreement from your committee) will appeal to the voters. Talk exclusively about those three issues. Become identified with those three issues. Hammer away at those three issues to the point of exhaustion (as far as your campaign staff is concerned).

If issues are to be addressed in your advertising, stress those three issues only.

If you are asked in your public appearances about issues other than your "holy trinity," you of course can respond because of the study you have done of all the issues. People will react positively because you are so well-informed.

Never become a one-issue candidate. If people are not concerned about the issue, you will lose. Three primary issues seems about the right number. It gets you beyond the one-issue problem and yet does not spread you so thin that you have no identity. Many voters may have only a passing interest in the office you seek; if they have any interest at all, you have a better chance of drawing their attention if you are talking about three issues. One of them may hit a nerve. If you are giving equal weight to twenty issues, there is a good chance that the voters will never take the time or trouble to sort them all out — you must sort them out first. As a citizen deeply involved in public affairs, you may find that attitude disappointing, but I am afraid that's the way it is.

Think back to campaigns you followed with some interest in the past. Can you recall more than three important issues in those campaigns?

A campaign with too many themes results in none of them being remembered. Your favorite television show uses the same opening theme every week. What would happen if the show had a different theme each week for twenty weeks? The chances are you would not remember any of them, even if they were recycled every twenty weeks.

The issues you select should not be ones that are too complicated to lend themselves to a sound campaign strategy. If you cannot come up with a meaningful one-sentence description of your position, it is too complicated to be included in the three issues you emphasize. That does not mean that you won't discuss that complicated issue if you have to, but you should not emphasize that issue.

If you can take a complicated issue and reduce it to some simple statements, then you might be able to include that issue, but be careful. A complex issue that is improperly reduced to too-simple statements may border on demagogy.

In selecting your issues, do not pick those that could be

turned against you. For example, you do not want to be identified as the "sewer candidate." That could happen if you make
sewers an issue to the exclusion of other matters. If it is one of
three subjects, there is less chance that you will become known
as the "sewer candidate." Similar issues such as garbage collec-
tion can be turned against a candidate, suggesting him to be
trite, no matter how significant the issue might really be.

In other words, at least one of your three issues ought to be
one you can sink your teeth into.

You may get tired of talking about these three issues. But remember that the people listening are probably hearing you
speak about them for the first time, so you have to sound fresh
and alive. Do not condense your discussion to the point that
you leave out important ingredients. A candidate speaks on
the same subjects so often that he soon believes people know
as much about them as he or she does and condensation sets
in. He may lose the effectiveness of his issue if he assumes that
his audience understands a great deal about it. His job as a
candidate is to educate them to his point of view.

You do need to simplify the issue, but without talking down
to the audience. You should never preface statements with a
remark such as, "Let me simplify it for you." That is talking
down to an audience and they will rightfully resent it. Instead
you should say, "I'm sure that you are aware . . . " or "I apologize to this audience for oversimplifying this issue, but I think
we need to keep it in its proper perspective." Assume that
some in the audience do not understand, but that some do.
Preface your remark for the benefit of those who may be
knowledgeable—this has a positive impact on the entire audience.

Talking about the issues without sounding either simple or
superior is the objective. Let's face it, it is just possible that it is
the people in government who take simple questions and turn
them into complex nightmares.

Part III

Fund Raising

13

Personal Solicitation

AN EFFECTIVE METHOD OF FUND raising is personal solicitation. It usually involves a group of friends of the candidate personally calling on people that they think will give sizable amounts to the campaign.

The first thing that is needed is a list of people who are to be called on. The basic list should come from the candidate. The candidate can list all of his friends and associates who are likely to give and should be solicited with a personal call.

Such a potential contributor list is expanded with names of people connected with the campaign along with an assessment of the amount that they should be asked to contribute. One of the concerns of many finance chairmen is that some people who could easily give $500 to the campaign will be asked for (and will give) only $100. Few contributors will give more than they are asked.

Some so-called political experts feel that people are complimented when you ask them for more money than they can possibly give. This may be true if you are asking someone for $500 and the most they can give is $100. However, if you ask a man for $1,000 when the biggest contribution he has ever made to any cause was twenty-five dollars, he may be indignant. And your committee obviously has not done a very good job of identifying the prospects.

In forming a contributor list, bear in mind those individuals who may conduct business with the office the candidate is seeking. Some people who do business with that office may gladly make a contribution, feeling it will be to their advantage to have someone in office who has received their campaign contribution. You have to decide from whom you are going to accept contributions.

Before individuals solicit money for your campaign, they should be financially committed themselves. An individual who does not give of his own money does not make an effective solicitor — he cannot very well convince someone else that they ought to do something that he is unwilling to do. It should be known right up front that those doing the asking have already been asked and have responded positively.

Do not ask any one individual to make too many calls. If you ask someone to call on ten people there is a good chance the calls will be made. If you expect him to call on fifty people it is doubtful the task will be successfully accomplished. One of the main responsibilities of a finance chairman is to see that such personal solicitations are properly organized so that everyone involved has only a manageable amount of work to do.

The candidate can very well participate in this fund raising, but it depends on the candidate. Some candidates loathe asking for money. They consider it demeaning or feel it puts them in a situation where a contributor might be embarrassed because he cannot give a large gift. Other candidates feel that they should not ask volunteers to do a task that they themselves are unwilling to do. In any case, the candidate does need to get involved with the people who will do the soliciting.

Decide how you are going to tie the campaign issues or philosophies into the fund raising. You obviously are not going to solicit funds from people who support the opposite side of the issues. Identify those people who are likely to agree with the positions you have taken. There may also be groups of people who will be inclined to give financial support if they are asked. If they cannot give as a group, they may provide you with a list of their membership and tell you who is likely to contribute.

Personal solicitation can be an effective way of raising funds for a political campaign. It is used in nearly every political campaign. One word of caution about this method of fund raising. It is usually employed early in the campaign to raise the initial funds. But perhaps a fund-raising dinner is to be held later. There will be hard feelings when an individual gives a substantial gift early in a campaign and later finds that additional money must be contributed toward a fund-raising dinner. If you are likely to schedule such a dinner later in the campaign, decide that early contributors who give more than a certain amount will be given a ticket to the dinner without an additional contribution. It will save you a lot of ill will. The counterargument is that if you hold a fund-raising dinner late in the campaign, it is a clear device to raise money—some of it from the same people. There are a few people, however, who give substantial amounts who do not care about going to a dinner. You have to decide which method of fund raising is applicable to your campaign situation.

14

The Fund-Raising Dinner

THE FUND-RAISING DINNER IS ONE of the most common forms of generating political campaign money. One of the first decisions to be made is the price to charge for the dinner. The price must be high enough so that it will generate the kind of money you need, but not so high that it will prohibit people from attending.

Once you decide on a dinner and a price, a dinner chairman should be appointed. In most cases, the dinner chairman works under the direction of the finance chairman. Of course you must select a place and a date. Selecting the place and size of the room is important. If you are expecting two hundred people to buy tickets, do not put them in a ballroom which seats one thousand people. You could meet your goal, but the dinner would look like a failure to those in attendance and to the news media covering the event. If you are expecting two hundred people, you are better off holding the dinner in a room that seats one hundred eighty people comfortably, but can squeeze in the two hundred.

Your dinner chairman will need a committee to help with the details. The most important part of that committee will be the group that sells the tickets — without ticket sales it does not matter how well the rest of the committee functions. Some of the points made in the chapter about personal solicitations also apply to selling tickets. Some campaigners feel that it is easier to sell tickets to a political dinner than it is to get outright contributions. Large contributors may buy blocks of tickets. If the room is arranged with tables that seat eight to ten people, potential large givers can be asked to buy an entire table.

Most people coming to these dinners will buy one or two tickets. You have to decide whether a ticket will cost $100, admitting two people, for example, or fifty dollars for one person.

It is my opinion that holding a fund-raising dinner for $25 per person that costs you $20 per person is not a fund-raising dinner at all — it is a political rally being held to generate enthusiasm for the candidate. From the campaign treasurer's perspective, you would be better off getting a $10 contribution from the same people.

A good rule of thumb to follow for a fund raiser: You ought to earn at least two dollars toward the campaign for every dollar the function costs you. In other words, if you can hold the dinner for $10 per person, you ought to be charging at least $30 per person.

There are several opinions about the quality of the meal to be served at fund-raising dinners. One theory is that people going to a fund-raising dinner expect and want most of the money to go to the campaign and not some hotel or restaurant. If this is correct, then you ought to minimize the expenditure on food, decorations, and entertainment.

The other theory contends that if people are paying a price three or four times what the meal is worth, they expect an adequate meal for their contribution; they will feel that the campaign committee and the candidate are taking unfair advantage of their generosity by serving an inadequate meal.

I feel that there is some truth in both positions and the outcome depends on the price. Someone spending a modest amount does not expect a banquet—he knows it is a fund raiser. However, someone spending a large amount, say $100 or more, expects a decent dinner in return for his contribution. You can get by with a bean feed at $20 if you advertise it as such—but do not have a bean feed for $100 without informing the guests, if you want to keep those supporters for the future.

If a cocktail party precedes the dinner you may have a cash bar. You can get by with this if the ticket price is modest. However, if you feel that you are charging the limit on the ticket price, then you'd better not push your luck by also having a cash bar. Either include a couple of cocktails with the price of the dinner or skip cocktails completely.

A program should be planned for the fund-raising dinner. A clergyman of some denomination is usually invited to these functions to give the invocation and benediction. (I suspect that the reason Roman Catholic clergymen appear at so many of these events is because the dinner chairman knows he only has to give away one dinner ticket, whereas if he invites a Protestant minister or a rabbi he will probably have to give tickets to the clergyman and his spouse.)

Scheduling a speaker other than the candidate is done for a purpose. If it is a prominent speaker, that speaker will help sell tickets. Equally important, the speaker (usually a politician) can say flattering things about your candidate that the candidate cannot say about himself (if he has any degree of humility). A dinner is a good time to hear a speaker from outside the area. (You will recall that an expert is defined as someone from out-of-town.) Such a speaker will add prestige to the event that you might not be able to achieve with a local speaker, unless that local speaker is someone whose fame has spread beyond your hometown.

It is easier to get an out-of-town speaker if you are running for an office on a partisan ticket. The local party officers can help to obtain such a speaker. Usually a political figure does not expect a fee for helping a fellow politician but he does expect his expenses to be paid (out of the dinner proceeds). If the speaker is coming by plane find out what the air fare is in advance and either send him the ticket or present him with a check for the air fare shortly after he arrives. Arrange for the hotel to bill your campaign committee so that when he checks out he is told the bill is taken care of.

Of course you should arrange transportation. Often speakers are picked up coming into town, but after the event they must find their own way to the airport.

Some basic procedures should be followed regarding the facilities and the program. Take nothing for granted about the facilities. Too often, the dinner committee assumes that because the hotel or restaurant has a lot of large dinners its staff knows how to handle such functions. The hotel or restaurant management too often figures its reputation depends on the food and how it is served. This is important, but at a political dinner it is not as important as the show you are putting on. A fund-raising dinner is a show and you ought to approach it as though you are producing a night of entertainment.

Here are some factors about any dinner, and political dinners in particular, that should be helpful.

1. *The public address system.* Do not wait until the night of the event to see if the public address system is working. If you discover it is inadequate for the event it is entirely too late to do anything about it. Surprisingly, many multimillion-dollar facilities are serviced by $14.95 public address systems. Listen to the system several days or weeks before your dinner. Take someone with you. One of you should speak into the microphone and the other should walk around the room and listen for any dead spots. Listen at a volume that is comfortable for you—then remember that you are listening to it in an empty room. Now find out how much higher you can turn it without getting feedback.

Does this system sound tinny or does it sound like the speaker's voice is coming from the bottom of a barrel? Can it be adjusted so that the voice sounds natural? See if you can arrange to hear the system with a full crowd in the room. Usually, an-

other convention chairman or banquet manager will be agreeable to your coming in and standing in the back of the room
for a few minutes during someone else's dinner so that you can
hear the sound system. If the room and food are exactly what
you are after but the public address system is a loser, consider
bringing in a rented public address system for your event.

Also check out the location of the microphone for the
speaker. Is it located on the lectern? Is it movable so that the
speaker can stand comfortably behind the lectern and have the
microphone adequately cover his voice? A mike on a floor
stand is usually not as comfortable.

There is nothing worse than having a great program that
half of the audience cannot hear. It is unfair to the speaker
and it is certainly unfair to the members of the audience who
parted with their hard-earned money to come to your dinner.

2. *Lighting.* Most people think lighting is just to see with;
they are not aware that a dinner can be successful with the help
of proper lighting. In many facilities a room is lit as though a
night baseball game were to be played there. It is lit for the
people working there rather than for the customers being
served.

The lighting over people should be adequate so that they can
see, but not so bright that they are sitting in the middle of a
floodlight. Candles on the table usually help. Lighting at the
head table is especially crucial for the speaker. Make certain
that there is a light on the lectern so that the speaker can see his
notes without glare. Make certain that there are spotlights on
the head table that can be focused on the lectern, so that everyone in the audience can see the speaker. An amber light is best,
as that is the most flattering color to skin tones. If amber is not
available use white. Never use green or blue as those colors on
the face of your speaker will make him look embalmed for a
Grade B horror movie.

3. *Elevation of head table.* The head table should be ele-
vated so that it is easily seen from every location in the room.
For the kind of dinner we are discussing a twelve- to eighteen-

inch elevation ought to do the job. If the dinner will be attended by thousands of people in a large auditorium, you could even set the head table on a stage. (Who ever said a political dinner wasn't show business?)

There are three reasons for recommending a twelve- to eighteen-inch elevation. First, it's not so high that people sitting in front are going to have to strain their necks all evening. Secondly, you are likely to have some people seated at the head table who are not used to sitting there. If it is too high they will feel as though you have put them on a pedestal and they will be just plain uncomfortable. The third reason is that people are too often taking a backward step off an elevation and taking a fall. You minimize the danger if the riser is not too high.

4. *Programs.* Printed programs at each table place setting let people know the agenda for the evening. People like to know what is going to happen. The program does not have to be elaborate, although it can be if the campaign can afford it. State the starting time and then start on time. There is something to be said for printing the approximate adjournment time, but do it only if you know you can control the time and can come close to meeting the objective.

5. *Music.* Music certainly adds a festive element to the dinner but can add greatly to the cost. I have known of dinners where the group played during the cocktail party, during the meal, and even for dancing afterwards. Sometimes an organist will play during the cocktail hour and dinner.

6. *Freebies.* A few tickets may have to be given away, but remember, this is a fund-raising dinner — it is not a charitable affair to reward all the faithful volunteers and paid staff. You will have to give complimentary tickets to members of the news media if you want them covering the event. It is also a good idea to have a reserved table for media people close to the head table so that they can do a decent job of reporting. The news media should know of the dinner well in advance. When you call the various medias with the date of your dinner,

ask if they are aware of any other events for that date that might create a conflict.

7. *Clearing the tables.* Have an understanding with the hotel or restaurant that tables will not be cleared once the program begins. There is nothing more disconcerting to a speaker than to try to do a great job while waiters, waitresses, and bus boys and girls go through an auditorium like a horde of locusts. Arrange this clearing of the tables ahead of time — if the management wants to clear before the speech has begun, they will have to do it with great dispatch.

8. *The order of serving the meal.* At nearly every banquet ever held, the head table has been served first. This means these diners finish first, and then sit at the head table watching the rest of the crowd eat. The master of ceremonies tries to look over the room to see when the man in the corner whose table was served last has finished eating so that the program can begin.

Everyone knows that the head table is served first as a matter of respect or courtesy. Banquets or dinners with a program following would be run much more efficiently if the head table was served last. You would probably have to make an announcement to the audience to go ahead and eat their meal when it was served because they are so used to having the head table served first. The advantage of having the head table served last is that the starting time of the program is no problem — when the head table finishes eating, everyone else should also be finished and the program may begin. However, it is difficult to get hotels and restaurants to make this kind of change in their operation.

9. *Controlling time.* Have the program timed. When you ask people to speak, let them know how long you want them to speak. Speakers will usually respect your time requests. Most audiences would prefer that a dinner be over before they expected than to sit there into the wee hours of the morning. The dinner chairman controls the time by his choice for master of ceremonies.

10. *The master of ceremonies.* This person should realize that he or she is primarily an expeditor. The master of ceremonies is not the show—he or she is there to see that things run smoothly. The agenda should be strictly followed. Too often an MC thinks it is his job to be the clown of the evening. The MC is there to make everyone else look good. If some humor can be interspersed into the program by the MC, that is fine if it is appropriate to the occasion. But to stand up and tell jokes is not the duty of an MC unless he is a professional and understands exactly what is going on. An MC never should tell a joke that anyone in the crowd might find offensive. If there is any doubt he should not tell the story.

11. *The role of the candidate.* The primary function of the candidate at such a dinner is to meet and greet people. If the candidate is to speak, what he says and how long he talks will depend on whether he is the principal speaker or if a guest speaker is playing that role.

If there is a guest speaker, it is often the responsibility of the candidate to introduce that guest. The candidate does not have to give a typical campaign speech because the guest will be there to convince everyone of the importance of electing the candidate. He or she should take a few minutes to express appreciation to the supporters and workers who are present. These are your friends—they do not have to be convinced of your qualifications. Therefore they should be addressed as "insiders," not rank-and-file voters you are trying to win over. Incidentally, these fund-raising dinners, when scheduled at a crucial time, can do wonders for the volunteers working on the campaign. It reinforces their judgment that they are working for the right candidate.

A paraphrased talk to a group of supporters at such a fund-raising dinner that the author recently heard follows:

"You don't know what it means to me to see all of you here tonight. This is the group that I really have counted on from the very beginning. I go back a long way with many of you in this room tonight. Many of you encouraged me to run back in the days when I was considering whether or not to be a candidate. One of the thoughts that goes through your mind when you're thinking about running for public office is will these people really get behind me and support me if I run? That question has been answered time and time again by friends such as you. We still have a long way to go in this campaign. I pledge to you that I will continue to work hard in this campaign. I'm going to continue to fight for the issues that you and I consider important. Whether or not I am elected may not be as important as the fact that you have been involved and have been so dedicated to my candidacy. I am confident that by our continued working together between now and election day we will win. We will bring to the voters the kind of dedication and concern they rightfully deserve."

One most important reminder about the fund raiser: All of the plans mean nothing if you do not sell a sufficient number of tickets. That is the number-one priority.

15

Direct Mail

CAMPAIGN MONEY CAN BE RAISED by direct mail, but it is not a simple task. There are two ingredients that are essential to raising money with a letter. The first is finding the right names to solicit, and the second is composing the letter itself.

A fund-raising letter sent to every voter in your area will probably be too costly and its return too uncertain. The only exception might be if you are running for an office that has quite a small area or a small number of voters. A precinct or a ward in some parts of the country might be small enough for you to send a fund-raising letter to every registered voter.

Your best bet is to solicit people for funds who have a record of contributing to political campaigns. The question is where to gather a list of such people. There are several sources.

1. If you have friends who hold office or who have run for office (even if unsuccessfully) they might make their list of contributors available to you.

2. Go the the library and read newspaper accounts of past races for the office you seek. Many times these stories will list the major contributors to all of the candidates.

3. In campaigns (most of them) that require contributions to be reported, find out where these reports are filed. Some

hints: city election reports may be filed with the city clerk; county race reports might be filed with a county clerk or county election commissioner; state races may be filed with the secretary of state. Be careful. Some jurisdictions prohibit such lists being copied for the purpose of soliciting for contributions. Make sure you know the law before you proceed.

4. Political parties may make their lists of contributors available to you. Often times in a partisan race, a party will not make a list available until after you have won the primary and you are their candidate. The reason is that they do not want their contributors deluged with requests for money from "outsiders." They should also be able to provide you with a list of people outside of your voting area who might contribute.

5. Have your key supporters make a list of people they believe might contribute to the campaign. Include in this list everybody who is working on the campaign. Every time you have a function that large numbers of people attend, have them register their address and phone number. Put them on your fund-raising letter list.

6. The candidate should make a list of everyone he or she thinks can and will contribute. Don't put people on the list for a mail solicitation if they should be personally solicited. You would have the problem we discussed earlier of people contributing a considerably smaller amount than they are capable of giving.

7. Organizations may make a list of their membership available to you. How you handle such lists is important. There needs to be a reason why the list is of some value to you. Getting a list of the local members of a fraternal organization may be important if the candidate is a member, or if that group is interested in the same issue that the candidate has stressed. Sometimes a member of an organization or even an officer will provide a membership list. Most organizations, however, are very sensitive about being involved in political campaigns. The reason is obvious—they may have members on all sides and they don't want to offend any of their mem-

bers by becoming embroiled in political controversy. If the candidate is a member, he may feel perfectly comfortable addressing a letter to "my fellow Elk." If he is not a member and is merely using the list, he probably should not even mention the fact that the letter is being addressed to members of the organization, but touch on issues that he believes will interest those members and will loosen the purse strings in the direction of his campaign.

8. Use lists of union members or chamber of commerce members. Such a list can be valuable particularly if you've taken positions their membership is likely to support. You may or may not be able to get these lists. You have to decide which groups you will pursue.

9. A recent explosion on the political scene is the emergence of political action committees (PACS), many having money to give candidates. Some of these groups are only interested in certain kinds of races. For instance an educational PAC might not be as interested in a city council race as it would a school board race. Most of the PACS (as of this writing) are interested in federal and, to a lesser degree, state-wide races. This could be changing, however.

Let's now discuss fund-raising letters. Letters should be targeted to the audience you are addressing. There may be a general fund-raising letter that goes to people we mentioned in items 1–6. Items 7–9 may require individually designed letters aimed at a specific interest group.

There are contradictory theories on fund-raising letters. One is that the letter should be brief and never go beyond one page, one side only. The other theory is that you should take as much space and paper as needed to go into great detail on issues and consequently generate financial support. Most candidates believe in and use the one-page concept, but several presidential candidates have raised enormous amounts of money with lengthy letters.

Since the overwhelming evidence supports the one-page concept, let's address ourselves to this approach. Too often a fund-raising letter comes across as cold and stiff. The people writing it spend too much time and effort with every word and phrase. They work it and rework it until it loses all of its spontaneity. It should be written as though the candidate were having a brief conversation with a potential financial supporter. One way the candidate can draft such a letter is to mentally visualize himself asking someone for money and having only about ninety seconds to get the message across.

The candidate doesn't have to write the letter if someone else on the campaign committee is more skillful at writing. But the letter's content should be something the candidate feels completely comfortable saying. If words or phrases are used that the candidate would not use, they should be changed. This assumes that the letter is to carry the candidate's name as the writer. If the letter is going to carry someone else's name, then different statements can be made. Very flattering things can be said about the candidate that he could never say about himself.

A fund-raising letter has only two primary functions—to obtain support, and to obtain money from the person reading it. Any other benefit generated from the letter is a bonus. The letter must be designed to meet these two primary functions. It is obvious that you should send these letters only to people you believe are inclined to be favorable to the candidate, the issues he articulates, and his candidacy.

A typical fund-raising letter from the candidate follows:

Dear Mr. and Mrs. Voter,

As a knowlegeable citizen I am sure you are aware that I have declared my candidacy for the city council.

There are important issues facing the citizens of our city this year. A copy of the statement I issued at the time I announced my candidacy is enclosed. I hope you will share my concern about these vital issues.

I would like to ask for your support in two ways.

One — as an influential person in the community, would you tell your friends about my candidacy and encourage them to support me?

Two — would you support my candidacy with your financial help? If we are to make my viewpoints known to the voters of this community, it will take money for campaign materials and media space and time.

A self-addressed envelope is enclosed for your reply. May we hear from you by the fifteenth?

Best regards,
(Signature)
Candidate

Let's analyze the above letter. You can make your letter much more specific if you like. In this letter, the content is quite nonspecific because a copy of the announcement statement would be included in the mailing.

Other items could be substituted for the candidacy announcement. You could use a favorable newspaper story that was published when you announced your candidacy. Or if there has been a newspaper editorial that makes some very favorable statements about you, that could be enclosed.

The advantage of enclosing another piece is that it can usually be included without increasing the postage costs. You could even enclose a campaign brochure if you have one at this point in the campaign, though a large brochure might increase your postage costs.

Always enclose a self-addressed envelope. I do not think you have to put postage on it because these people know you are trying to raise money and they won't mind (in most cases) providing their own stamp. You can print a statement in the upper-right hand side of the return envelope in a square equal to the size of a postage stamp which says, "Your stamp here helps too!"

The letter written by someone other than the candidate can be more glowing in its praise of the candidate, but it shouldn't be laid on too thick. Here is an example of a letter for the same candidate that carries the name of the campaign chairman and the finance chairman:

Dear Mr. and Mrs. Voter,

The two of us would not get involved in a campaign for the city council if we did not feel deeply about the issues and a candidate.

We feel that there are crucial issues facing the voters of this city in this election. The quality of people serving on our city council could determine the quality of life in our community for the next decade and even beyond.

We encouraged Joe Brown to run for this office. He gave it consideration for a period of time in a logical, thoughtful way that is typical of him. After studying all sides of the question, he decided that he would run. We were delighted because it isn't often that a person of Joe's experience and qualifications runs for our city council. Joe has an ability to cut through all of the extraneous material and get to the heart of the issues. That quality is rare indeed and sorely needed on our city council. A copy of a newspaper story about Joe is enclosed.

We would not ask you to do something that we have not already done ourselves. We both have made our contributions to Joe's campaign. If we are going to have this qualified citizen sitting on our city council, it will require your support and your money.

Won't you please use the enclosed return envelope to send Joe your campaign contribution?

We look forward to hearing from you by the fifteenth so that Joe and the campaign committee can formulate the plans that will bring victory in this crucial election.

> Best regards,
> (Signature)
> Campaign
> Chairman
>
> (Signature)
> Finance
> Chairman

In both letters we asked for a return by a specified date. If you leave this open-ended, people do not get the feeling of urgency. If individuals are sympathetic to your candidate, a good many of them will send checks by that date. Others who may want to make a contribution but cannot pay by the date you requested may phone and tell you that they will contribute but cannot make it by your date.

If this is a quality solicitation list, your workers could start making followup phone calls about five days after the deadline.

Some campaigns have had success by enclosing pledge cards similar to those that many churches use for their member canvass. The advantage is that people may pledge to pay more over a period of five or six months than they would pay if they have to write the check immediately. One of the problems with the pledge card approach is that it does not provide the money you need up front. This can be solved by having the pledge card show when installments will be paid. Another disadvantage is that the campaign committee has to organize followup procedures to collect the pledges.

Sometimes campaign committees cannot resist the temptation to make the pledge card serve many purposes. Instead of restricting it to soliciting money, they will also ask if you wish to work on the campaign, help raise money, put up a campaign yard sign, go door to door in your precinct, or mail post cards on behalf of the candidate to twenty-five of your friends.

You should avoid the temptation to make the pledge card a multipurpose one. It allows people to rationalize a smaller contribution by also checking some other activity on the card. Do not confuse the issue — the objective of a fund-raising letter is to raise money. Providing people with a rationalization device is counterproductive.

Raising money by mail is more difficult than generating it with personal visitations. It is too easy to lay a letter aside. A fund-raising letter sent to a quality list of potential supporters, followed by a phone reminder, however, can be effective.

16

The Fund-Raising Cocktail Party

A FRIEND OF MINE ONCE devised a unique fund-raising cocktail party. For $25 you were entitled to come to the cocktail party to meet and visit with the candidate. For $50 you did not have to attend the event, so you did not have to meet and visit the candidate. Unfortunately it never caught on.

There are two kinds of fund-raising cocktail parties — those with advance ticket sales, and those without.

Cocktail Party With Advance Ticket Sales

This kind of fund raiser is similar to a fund-raising dinner in that you sell tickets and people attend the event. However, it is much less formal. No meal is served and people mill around, and come and go at various times. Even though a cocktail party may be scheduled, say from 7:00 to 9:00 P.M., people are not expected to remain for the entire period. They drift in and drift out. If you plan on having the candidate address the group, you might print on the tickets, "Brief remarks by Candidate Smith at 8:00 P.M." That way if people do want to hear the candidate speak they know what time they need to be there.

The advantage of these cocktail parties is that you can hold quite a few of them. You can usually get some solid supporter to offer his or her home for the event. He might even furnish the cocktails and hors d'oeuvres. However if he does, make sure you know the reporting laws; in some elections the value of the cocktails and hors d'oeuvres furnished might have to be reported as an in-kind contribution.

If one of your supporters will provide the residence, cocktails, and hors d'oeuvres, then the ticket sales are receipts for the campaign. By nature cocktail parties are considered friendly, intimate gatherings and should not be very large. I cannot recommend them in place of a fund-raising dinner, but they can be a great supplement to a dinner.

The ticket price for a cocktail party will depend on the kind of list you can pull together. The real magic ingredient in fund raising is to know the right amount to ask for. Asking for too little is a problem as is asking for too much.

Cocktail Party Without Advance Ticket Sales

The cocktail party without advance ticket sales is intended to raise the money from the people after they have arrived. It is important that these people know when they are invited that the purpose is to raise money for the candidate. If you don't make it unmistakably clear, people may feel trapped or embarrassed.

You need to feel fairly certain that these people are favorably inclined toward your candidate before you invite them. You can stand a few who may be neutral about your candidate, but you do not want to risk inviting anyone who is supporting your opponent. That kind of person at a fund-raising cocktail party can discourage some neutral attendees who might otherwise be inclined to contribute.

The candidate attends this cocktail party because the people invited are people who are capable of making sizable contributions.

Let's assume that this cocktail party is scheduled to last two hours—from 7:00 to 9:00 P.M. The candidate spends the first hour visiting informally with the potential contributors. The candidate does not talk to them about money, unless someone specifically asks about the campaign's finances. The candidate talks about the campaign and the issues and works on establishing the one-on-one relationships that develop strong supporters.

During the cocktail party, the candidate should try to visit personally with everyone in attendance, so that each person feels that the candidate has paid some attention to him.

It is difficult for a candidate who is distant and aloof to fare well in this kind of campaigning. If he comes off as a "cold fish" this kind of technique should be avoided. Some candidates who come across very well in a formal speech, and may even appear to be warm and comfortable, are actually loners by nature and do not do well in a one-on-one situation. You must recognize what kind of commodity you are packaging.

At 8:00 P.M. the campaign chairman or the host of the cocktail party (decide in advance) introduces the candidate, who talks to the group for approximately ten minutes. The candidate can speak about the campaign and the three issues that he is emphasizing.

The candidate's talk might be ended with a statement similar to the following:

"I want to thank Dave and Fran for their generosity in hosting this cocktail party tonight. They are dear friends and their support means a great deal to my candidacy. I have another campaign commitment tonight, but we all know that you were invited here this evening, not only so we could visit, but so you could be asked to support our campaign financially. Someone will be discussing that with you tonight. I want to thank you for all you have done, for what you are doing and for whatever financial support you might decide on tonight. One thing we have discovered in this campaign is that the demands upon our time are plentiful, so as much as I would like to stay for the rest of the evening, I must move on. Thank you so much for being here. Good night."

The candidate should leave so that others can make a strong pitch for financial support. The candidate's closing remarks do not require much explanation. Everyone knows that the candidate is aware that they were invited so that their financial support could be solicited. Incidentally, paying a great deal of attention to the people who are hosting the party is important — it builds them up with their friends and indicates a close relationship with the candidate. That kind of recognition never hurts anyone.

When the candidate leaves, the finance chairman (or someone selected for his effectiveness in raising money) will make the pitch for campaign contributions. The talk might go something like this:

"I am very impressed with the quality of our candidate for the office of _____ . I am sure that all of you are as impressed as I have been. Many of us in this room have said that we wished better qualified candidates would seek these offices. Well, we got our wish. We have a super candidate and now we have the chance to support him. I am pledging a contribution tonight of $500 (or whatever the appropriate amount should be) and I ask all of you to fill out one of these cards before you leave here tonight."

At this point the cards could be passed out to everyone in attendance. If you prefer, and if you think it is appropriate, you can have two or three people preprogrammed to get the support going. Someone you know who will contribute to the campaign can make a statement aloud that he will support the candidate, and then write out his personal check right on the spot.

I have known of campaigns where this type of "shill" approach is carried too far — the shill never actually makes a gift, but is just used to coax others to give. Such a person may attend fifteen or twenty fund-raising cocktail parties and submit the same "gift" to each one, with his check never being cashed. If your campaign is in such serious financial straits that you have to resort to that kind of dishonesty, you are in trouble. It is perfectly acceptable to have someone who is actually going to make a contribution to say so in a fund-raising situation — but to purposely mislead people into believing something that is not actually happening is hoodwinking your supporters. If you will do that to them during a campaign, you will do it to them as an office holder.

Have a list available of everyone attending and when the evening is over check those who contributed against the list. In this case, I do not believe you have to follow up with people who do not contribute. The reason they were invited was obvious, the message given was obvious, and so unless they volunteer some excuse such as "I forgot my check book," I do not believe you need to follow up. These people have said no.

Several of these cocktail parties can raise a great deal of money for the campaign. They use a lot of the candidate's time, but are one of the most important functions in the campaign.

One more idea, not only for cocktail parties, but for any campaign gathering — always provide name tags for people when they enter. If you can have the tags prepared in advance, that is even better. The name tag's primary use in a campaign is to save the candidate the embarrassment of forgetting someone's name. It also helps for the guests to become acquainted with each other.

17

Professional Entertainers and Celebrity Fund-Raising Performances

PERFORMANCES BY ENTERTAINERS AND CELEBRITIES for fund-raising purposes have been used more and more in recent years. First you have to explore the possibility of getting a celebrity to offer your campaign a hand. Both the Democratic National Committee and the Republican National Committee have a list of celebrities or performers who are willing to help candidates of each particular party. The circumstances under which they will perform are known to the staff of each national committee. The best way to obtain this information is through your state party office. If the staff doesn't have the information, it is a simple matter for them to get it from the national office.

Some celebrities have a "cause." If they're deeply committed to their cause and it coincides with an issue that you support, you might convince them to help you. These people might be difficult to identify. For the most part you will have to depend on the regular media for this information.

Professional or celebrity campaign support is approached in a variety of ways. Some of these concepts will overlap to a degree, so please pardon what may appear to be duplication.

The Appearance That Coincides with
Another Performance

The best chance to get a celebrity to help your campaign exists if he or she is in your community for a performance and could also appear at your function. I do not believe you should approach a performer cold. Check with other sources to see if you are the type of candidate this performer supports or if you are on the same side of an issue that this performer is deeply committed to.

Most performers will not get involved in an activity that will compete with their primary commitments. Their first obligation is to the performance for which they are being paid. If an entertainer is in town to perform in the local concert hall for a fairly stiff price, he or she is not about to give a concert in the park that afternoon on behalf of your campaign. But a celebrity might agree to attend a fund-raising cocktail party on your behalf. If this is scheduled well enough in advance, you can sell tickets at a substantial price per person because there are people who will gladly pay to rub elbows and chat for a few moments with a celebrity.

Another opportunity could occur when a celebrity is in town for a performance the same evening you are having a function. The celebrity may be willing to put in a brief appearance at your function before moving on to the real purpose of his or her trip. The trouble with such "drop-ins" is that since you cannot count on them, you cannot use their presence to boost ticket prices. However, they may have some news value, perhaps enough for a story and some photos of the celebrity and the candidate.

Few celebrities will become involved in a local campaign unless it involves an issue that they are committed to. They are more likely to become involved in a race for the Congress or perhaps the governorship of a state. Most who do get involved in such campaigns are politically active individuals who support one political party.

The Celebrity Who Appears Specifically for
Your Campaign

This is usually a situation in which a performer supports liberals, conservatives, Democrats, Republicans, or individuals who are committed to his pet cause. In this situation the celebrity will come into your community or state for the specific purpose of helping your campaign. The campaign committee pays for the performer's expenses.

Celebrities can be very helpful in raising money for your campaign. We already discussed how they could be utilized at a fund-raising cocktail party. They can also be most helpful at a fund-raising dinner. Their name and appearance will sell tickets. For some reason, people like to look at individuals that they have seen on television or on the movie screen.

The celebrity may make a few remarks at a fund-raising dinner, but you should not count on him or her for a principal speech, even though you may advertise the event that way. The final speech in such situations should be made by the candidate even though the celebrity may be a tough act to follow. A well-known performer is not necessarily a spellbinder as a speaker. The reason I believe the candidate should speak after the celebrity is so that people are again reminded of why they are there, which is to support the candidacy. It also gives the candidate the chance to thank the performer for the support which made the dinner a success.

Another approach that can be used involving a celebrity is to have a reception for the performer before the dinner itself. People invited to this reception are those who contribute more than a certain amount. For example, if your dinner ticket is going for $100 per couple, every couple contributing $500 will also receive an invitation to the celebrity reception where they will have the opportunity to meet the performer.

I have known this arrangement to be carried one step further, although I think most celebrities would object to it — everyone attending would be photographed with the celebrity.

Do not schedule any of these activities unless you have

cleared them with the celebrity or his or her agent well in advance. You could have a serious problem if you sell tickets to a reception that the performer refuses to attend.

The Performer

You are renting a hall and hiring a performer to put on a show. You sell the tickets and the amount you collect beyond what you owe is money for your campaign. Sounds simple? It isn't! Do not try it without some sound professional assistance. While some cynics might say there is little difference between show business and politics, there are facets of putting on performances that political people are not familiar with, and should not attempt to handle alone.

If you are considering this approach to fund raising, get professional help. If it is done with the right performer or performers, this type of event can generate a great deal of capital for your campaign treasury.

Visit a reputable local promoter who brings name performers into your community on a regular basis. He makes his living promoting such entertainments and should know what he is doing. There are contracts with the facility where the concert (or whatever) will be held. There is the contract with the performer. If there are supporting acts, there may also be contracts with the musicians union. An entertainment promoter will know how to handle all of these items.

There are several ways that the financial arrangements with entertainers are handled. One is a flat guarantee, another is a straight percentage of the gate, and the third is a combination of the two.

If an entertainment promoter is committed to your campaign, he might handle this affair for you as his contribution to the campaign, or he might do it at a nominal cost in comparison to what he would normally profit from such a performance. Or he might charge you his full price for this activity and it could very well be worth what it costs.

In my opinion you should never have such a function and charge a normal price for the performance. If you do that and everyone gets their normal percentage, you will receive nothing but the risk involved if the event is unsuccessful.

You need to charge an amount that will raise substantial funds for your campaign. You can usually charge at least as much as you would for a fund-raising dinner. Many people would rather pay a substantial amount and have an evening of professional entertainment than to go to a dinner and listen to political speeches.

Once you decide to go with this approach (after considering the risk and working with the professional promoter), the main responsibility of the campaign committee will be to see that tickets get sold. In that regard, it is not unlike selling tickets to a political dinner. It may even be easier, but it is still a tough job for one reason — human beings generally do not like to give away their money.

There is always the temptation for the candidate to get up on the stage and give a political speech at such an event. This is a mistake. If the candidate must speak at all, a good time to come on stage is right after the intermission. Thank everyone for being there, tell them how much it means to the support of the campaign, and then get off.

Another way of handling candidate recognition is for the campaign manager to make similar remarks and then introduce the candidate, who is seated out in the audience. As the spotlight beams down, he or she stands, waves to the crowd, and sits down.

Remember, a large portion of the crowd may be there primarily because they are fans of the entertainer. It is possible that they are not particularly interested in your campaign. They may be neutral about your candidacy, but if you eat into the time they believe they paid to be entertained, you may lose their votes. The primary purpose is to raise money for the campaign, and not for the candidate to get his kicks hearing the sound of his voice in front of a captive audience.

In conclusion, if you seriously consider going this route, get professional assistance, or you are likely to lose the family farm.

18

Other Methods of Fund Raising

THERE ARE OTHER METHODS OF raising money for political campaigns. Some of them are effective only in certain regions of the country, and might not work in every location.

Auctions

The type of auction that is most effective as a method of political fund raising is the "celebrity-donated item auction."

Well in advance of the auction, your campaign workers contact political celebrities to see if they will donate a personal item that could be auctioned. An example might be the president of the United States donating a necktie that he has worn. This assumes that the president is of the same political party and would help you. You might also approach well-known senators or congressmen for such items.

A typical list of possibilities would include:

1. Item of a personal nature donated by well-known political figures, or their relatives.

2. Items of a personal nature donated by show business celebrities.

3. Old rare campaign buttons (a good number of people collect campaign pins and buttons).

4. A donated first edition of a book autographed by the author.

5. Items of value donated by supportive business people.

6. Items the committee buys for the specific purpose of auctioning.

One of the biggest problems with an auction is deciding where and under what circumstances it will be held. Getting people out for an auction may be difficult; it requires some special kind of event to draw a group. If you combine it with a cocktail party and generate a party atmosphere, you will get more people to attend and probably get larger bids than you otherwise would. However, you cannot afford to provide free cocktails, but most people will not object to a cash bar.

If you can obtain a professional auctioneer to run your auction as a method of assisting the campaign, you will certainly make a lot more money from the auction than you would if an inexperienced friend agrees to fill in.

Garage Sales

These may be effective in some regions of the country. Supporters of your campaign donate items for a garage sale. One person offers the use of a garage where the sale can be held.

The advantage of a garage sale is that the price of everything sold is virtually clear as income to the campaign. The only expense involved is for the classified ads that need to run in the local newspapers advertising the sale.

There is some question as to whether or not you should advertise the garage sale as a political event. The reason for letting everyone know is that those people who support you will attend the garage sale who might not otherwise have come. It is also reasoned that under the circumstances people will be willing to buy things that are overpriced because they know the purpose of the garage sale.

A reason not to advertise the sale as a political fund-raising activity is that people who may be inclined to support your opponent will not come to a garage sale if they know it is a fund raiser for your political campaign. If it is simply advertised as a garage sale with some interesting items listed, people will come because they are looking for a bargain.

A garage sale is a good way to raise money because people enjoy having them. They have become an interesting semisocial event in some American suburbs. So it is important that these sales be conducted by those supporters of your campaign who have held a couple of successful garage sales. You can have several garage sales going on at the same time in various sections of the community. A surprising amount of money can be raised through garage sales.

Bake Sales

Bake sales can be used to raise small amounts of money for a campaign. Their primary benefit is that they give volunteers the opportunity to do something constructive for the campaign. People who cannot or will not go door-to-door will bake cakes and cookies. The biggest problem with bake sales is that you may have trouble finding a place to hold the sale. Supermarkets which will often allow church groups to sell their baked goods in their stores will not allow a political group to use their space because they are afraid of offending some customers.

The best opportunity for your people to sell these products is at a function of your own political party which is sympathetic to your need to raise money in various ways.

The primary value of bake sales is that they enable some people to feel that they are making a contribution to the campaign effort, and that's important for them.

Rummage Sales

Rummage sales are similar to garage sales except they are much, much larger. The concept of collecting items for a rummage sale follows the garage sale approach. Instead of holding the sale in someone's garage, you may consider renting a hall at a good location with adequate parking.

While you may run the ad in the garage-sale section of the classified ads, you should consider a larger type of display ad. It should be written to generate as wide an interest as possible. Of course you cannot advertise things you do not have, but you should emphasize the items which will generate traffic to your sale. Again depend on people from your campaign who have had rummage sale experience.

The reasons given in the section on garage sales about whether or not to advertise them as political fund raisers also apply to rummage sales.

Door-to-Door Solicitation

Door-to-door solicitation is not practical except as a byproduct of campaigning for votes. It is difficult to go door-to-door and get people to give you money for a political candidate. The main purpose in going door-to-door is to ask people for their support at the polls. Many people will resent your even coming to their door. However you are usually able to leave a brochure with the request that they consider voting for your candidate. You will occasionally come across someone who is positive about your candidate. When this happens you may be able to raise some money from that individual. You might say, "I compliment you on how knowledgeable you are about public affairs. We do not run into many people who take the trouble to study the candidates and the issues. As you know, it takes money to win elections. Would you also consider making a contribution to the campaign?"

You may collect a few dollars in this way. You certainly won't get them if you don't ask for them. But if you are not receiving some very positive vibrations from the person on the other side of that screen door, don't ask for the contribution because it may cost you a vote. The purpose of knocking on doors is to garner votes. The money you collect is a welcome byproduct. If the individual says that he can't give now but will later, give him a self-addressed envelope (without postage) and hope that it is used.

Television Solicitation

You don't run television ads for the purpose of raising money, but you might have a statement at the end of your ad which solicits campaign contributions and tells people where they can send their checks. Whether or not this will raise much money will depend on how deeply people feel about the issues and the candidates in your election.

Part IV

The Campaign

19

Scheduling the Candidate's Time

ONE PERSON IN THE CAMPAIGN must be in charge of the candidate's time schedule. This will eliminate the possibility of several people on the campaign committee agreeing to send the candidate to different places at the same time. The cancellation of an appearance creates a worse image than if the candidate had never accepted the date in the first place.

Early in the campaign you need to know how much campaigning the candidate can actually do and still appear fresh and create a favorable impression. If a candidate is spending all of his or her time running for the office, a different scheduling problem exists than if the candidate is working at a job full-time and restricting campaign appearances to evenings and weekends.

In scheduling time, you need to be aware of the kinds of campaigning the candidate likes to do and does well. If the candidate does not like going into a precinct to knock on doors and visit with people, then it is foolish to plan much of that type of activity — the candidate won't do it. Sometimes scheduling the type of campaigning that the candidate does very well is even more difficult. For example, if the candidate comes off particularly well speaking at dinners, there are only so many of such dinners available for him to address. Utilize that speaking ability in as many situations as you can arrange. In addition to accepting all political dinners, try also to get the candidate to address service groups that meet for luncheons. This is just an example of utilizing the strength of the candidate.

Is your candidate a morning or evening person? If the candidate is the type that bounces out of bed in the morning and is immediately operating at full speed, then this individual can be scheduled very early in the morning, such as greeting workers as they enter a plant. However, if your candidate is an evening person who can hardly speak until midmorning, and only after drinking four cups of coffee, you should not schedule early morning activities. Always place your candidate in the best possible light. The evening person should not be scheduled for many breakfast meetings. He does not like to be up that early, and so there is a strong likelihood that he won't perform as well as he would later in the day.

Also determine how much campaigning the candidate can do and still be effective. If the candidate runs out of gas after three or four hours of campaigning, then you obviously should not schedule six hours of solid campaigning.

People working on campaigns often do not realize how exhausting campaigning can be for some candidates. They believe that the more they can get the candidate out working, the better. You are better off with four solid hours of a fresh candidate than a twelve-hour day during which the candidate looks exhausted during eight of those hours.

Make certain that the candidate is well rested if you are going to be shooting film for future television ads or if you are going to be taping a television show.

Many candidates are exceedingly high-energy people who can go out and campaign vigorously for twelve hours, leaving staff and volunteers completely exhausted all along the way. It is interesting that there are so many high-energy people who seek public office. It is a good thing because many offices require that the office holder work long hours.

The effectiveness of the campaigning done is more important than following an exhaustive schedule to convince everyone how hard you all are working, especially if such scheduling is ineffective. This is one of the biggest problems that campaign workers face—they cannot be sure of what is effective so they feel they must do everything. Choosing one activity over another is always difficult because each activity usually has its advocates on the campaign team.

No hard and fast rule exists that you can follow about which activity is best for your candidate, because different types of campaigning are required in different parts of the country. But a general rule to follow is to utilize the campaign approaches that the candidate seems to perform naturally and enjoy the most (or dislike the least) if you are forced into choices. You are going to have a more impressive and spontaneous candidate with this approach.

20

Campaign Brochures
and Handouts

ONE PRINCIPLE THAT NEARLY EVERY campaign follows is that you need some kind of material to hand out to people when you are campaigning.

Campaign Brochures

The campaign brochure is used by more campaigns than almost any other approach. Brochures can be as simple as a small card or as elaborate as a booklet.

The most commonly used brochure is a four-page pamphlet consisting of one sheet of paper folded in the center with printing on the front and back.

The front page usually shows a very attractive photograph of the candidate with the name of the candidate and the office being sought. The campaign slogan might also be used on this cover page.

The two inside pages will be used to get your message across to the voters. Another photo could be used inside, but remember the more photographs you use, the more expensive the production costs will be. Often times the inside page will have a photo of the candidate's family. Never use the family picture on the front cover of the brochure unless the candidate is well known and easily recognizable. If that is not the case, a family photograph, especially one showing adult children, may leave the voter wondering which one is the candidate. By putting the candidate on the cover alone, the candidate then will be easily identified in the family group photograph.

The last page should repeat the main message of your campaign — it will make a double impression and will be the last thing the reader sees.

A fault of most brochures is that too much material is squeezed onto the space available. If the print is too small, with material covering every inch of the paper, you run the risk that most people will not read it. Therefore leave a lot of white space. If you have to err on the side of too little material or too much, lean toward too little material. You will have a much better chance that it will be read.

If you use color as opposed to black-and-white it will cost you more money. Consider the printing costs carefully. The larger the quantity, the less expensive each brochure. Depending on the kind of printing job ordered, you might find that the second five thousand brochures will cost a fraction of what the first five thousand cost. It becomes critical that you do an accurate job of estimating the number you will use. The second five thousand is a fraction of the cost of the first five thousand *only* if they are run by the printer at the same time.

Brochures are a great crutch for the candidate and campaigners. It gives them something to do with their hands. They do not have to give the campaign message orally. They can hand the voter a brochure.

Often the candidate will stand and greet voters at a street corner or shopping center. The candidate can shake hands with people, but that gets old pretty fast. If he does not want to shake hands, the situation becomes awkward. The brochure removes that uncomfortable feeling. If the candidate does not hand out brochures, people campaigning with him can hand them out. Those campaigning with the candidate should be attired with plenty of campaign material on their clothing or with campaign hats; people approaching will quickly see that this is a candidate for a political office rather than someone trying to sell them something or solicit them for a contribution to some obscure private organization.

There are so many different uses you can make of a brochure in a campaign that it becomes a basic tool. I believe that the brochure piece in a campaign is a must.

Campaign Cards

The campaign card serves much the same purpose as the brochure except it is much smaller and is of cardboard stock. You can put a photo and small message or campaign slogan on the front along with the office being sought.

The back of the card can be used for a variety of purposes. The candidate's qualifications or organizational memberships can be enumerated. The objectives the candidate plans to accomplish when elected could be printed.

Another interesting approach used by some candidates is to put some information on the back of the card that has nothing to do with the campaign, but which may be of sufficient interest to the recipients that they keep the cards permanently. There are a number of subjects you might use. Here are some examples.

1. The hunting season with all the various dates applicable.

2. A football schedule for the local team or teams.

3. A listing of all the counties in the state by license plate number.

4. Recipes.

5. Astrology signs with birth dates.

6. A list of the state's legal holidays.

7. The location and attractions at all state parks.

8. The list of all past presidents with their vice-presidents.

9. Little known historical facts about your community or state.

10. A list of all past governors of your state.

Matchbooks

Matchbooks are not used as campaign handouts as much as they used to be for several reasons. One is that many people are becoming nonsmokers; another is that no candidate wants anyone to be able to say that the fire at his house was started by children getting hold of the candidate's campaign book matches. One place that matchbooks are still used is at political dinners. A couple of books may be placed at every table in the ash trays.

Helium Balloons

You may want to give away helium-filled balloons at functions where there are large crowds, such as county and state fairs. Balloons with your candidate's name and office being sought can make a good impression. All children who see them want them, and a large number of kids accidentally let go of them and almost everyone will look up and watch them float away.

You can also give them away outside of football stadiums so that people will carry them in. However, some stadiums are beginning to forbid balloons with political advertising. So before you go to this expense, find out if balloons will be permitted inside the stadium. In some cities there is a tradition of letting balloons go skyward when the home team scores its first touchdown.

Emery Boards

Emery boards are handouts that many women will keep indefinitely. You can print messages on both sides. Their biggest drawback is that you cannot hand them out to men. However, they are kept by many women who receive them.

Campaign Buttons

Almost every campaign committee feels that it must have campaign buttons or pins. They are worn primarily by people who are deeply committed to the candidate. These supporters will wear the buttons constantly the last few weeks of the campaign. They become walking miniature billboards for the candidate. Because buttons or pins are so small, the message that can be placed on them is limited. The candidate's last name and the office being sought is about the extent of the lettering that can be placed on the pin.

Stick with the color scheme you are using for the campaign. Choose a color combination and stick with that all the way — do not use a different color combination for every piece of material. This is a decision that should be made early in the campaign. Make certain the colors will look good in the design of all campaign materials planned.

The biggest demand for buttons and pins comes from collectors. There are countless collectors now and a great percentage of your buttons will never be worn. It is difficult for a campaign committee to avoid buttons or pins. The demand is often the greatest from your own volunteers.

Campaigns are now using the small metallic-looking lapel button that spells out the name of the candidate. These are much more expensive than standard pins and are usually given only to those who contribute a specified amount. They can be purchased in gold or silver. They have been used often in presidential campaigns. Such a lapel pin can be worn on a suit without getting the garish look that goes with most campaign buttons.

21

Use of the Media

IT IS DIFFICULT TO GET your message across personally to every voter unless you are running for office in a small geographic area where every voter can be contacted either by the candidate or a member of the campaign committee. It is important to remember that no matter how effective other campaigners are, the voter is most interested in meeting and talking to the candidate.

Even in situations in which a great deal of personal campaigning takes place, you still need to reinforce it with other methods—namely, the use of the media.

A strange thing happens when people watch television. They consider anyone they see on television with regularity to be a celebrity. It does not matter if the "celebrity" is seen on a paid commercial. Why do you think so many automobile dealers appear on television to do their own commercials rather than hiring professional announcers who would do a far superior job? They do it as an ego trip and to build themselves into celebrity status within the community. It often works quite successfully.

If you are using an ad agency and if your race warrants that kind of expenditure, the agency may use television. I cannot recommend do-it-yourself television commercials—they look like home movies compared to professional ones. You should depend on your ad agency for the production and time to be selected.

There are ways to get some free coverage. When you are ready to announce your candidacy, you can call a press conference and invite all of the television stations, radio stations and newspapers. Pick a time of day that will enable these various medias time to get your news on their evening news show or in the evening paper.

An afternoon newspaper may have a 12:00 or 1:00 P.M. deadline for its early afternoon edition. A press conference called for 10:30 A.M. which ends in forty-five minutes does several things: it enables the evening newspaper reporter to make the deadline; it gives the television people plenty of time to get their video tape or film processed and edited and their story written for the early evening news. And there is a good chance that the story may be repeated in its entirety on the late evening news. It also gives the radio people, who will do an audio tape of your conference, the probability of getting it on their noon newscasts with a good chance of the entire expanded story being repeated on their early evening news.

If you have a mid-afternoon news conference you run the risk that it will not make the early evening news. It may get front page coverage in the morning paper (if there is one), but may only get brief notice on the evening newscasts because by then the news will be twenty-four hours old. Therefore the mid-morning press conference has many advantages.

If one newspaper staff is friendly to you and another is not, you may wish to time your press conference so that the friendly one gets to press with the story first. This is not true with television and radio, so you have to weigh the effect of your timing on their ability to run the story to full advantage.

When you call such a press conference to announce your candidacy, fill the room with campaign supporters. Make sure that the room is small enough that you can fill it. This crowd gives the television cameramen an audience to film. Reserve the first few rows (or at least one side of the first few rows) for the press.

At such an announcement press conference, always hand out a copy of your statement to the members of the media in advance. This makes it unnecessary for them to make hurried notes while you are speaking and reduces the chance that any part of your statement will be misquoted.

After you have read your statement, give the reporters the opportunity to ask questions. Often the questions may probe into some part of your official announcement statement. How you react at an early press conference may determine the kind of coverage you get in the entire campaign. You must get the media's respect; they won't respect you if they can intimidate you. Many reporters come on strong with what appears to be a very abrasive personality. Some mistake their freedom of the press as a license to disregard good manners. Some will see how far they can push you. Do not allow yourself to be pushed — often times, the pushing will stop the moment you push back. They know that as an office holder, you can make it difficult for them to get stories, so usually even the most obnoxious reporters won't push too far.

Answer the reporters' questions as honestly as you can, but do not allow yourself to be trapped into answering questions you do not know or do not want to answer at this point. If you do not know, you are better off saying, "I haven't taken a position on it yet, but I will during the campaign." If it is something that you do not consider relevant to the campaign, say so.

This kind of question and answer period tests your ability to think on your feet. As was suggested in an earlier chapter, make certain *in advance* that you can handle this type of situation.

You may have other opportunities during the campaign to call a press conference. If you call one for insignificant matters, you will lose credibility; the next one you call will remain virtually unattended. So make certain that you have something newsworthy to say before calling a press conference.

Another method of getting free media coverage is with press releases. You can issue a press release on the major campaign appointments. There is no sense in announcing them all at the same time — why put out one press release when five will do? Recognize that these announcements may not be carried by all of the media, but they will be used by some. Every time you can get your campaign mentioned, you get a bit of free advertising for your candidacy.

Such press releases also do a great deal for the morale of the people being appointed. They are seldom insulted by reading their name in the paper or by hearing it on television or radio.

Another method of obtaining free coverage is with statements on issues that are relevant to the campaign. They cannot be trivial matters or they will not get printed or mentioned on television or radio.

Make certain that the newspapers have an eight by ten inch official campaign photo. With some stories there is a chance they may use your photograph, but they cannot do it if they do not have a picture in their files. The same applies to the television stations; they may use your photo in a news story by showing it on the screen while the newscaster is reading the copy.

Often times radio (and occasionally television) stations are interested in having the candidate's voice making the statement or parts of it. The way to handle this is to add a note at the bottom of the press release: "For the candidate's voice recording of this statement or a part of it, phone _____." This means that for an hour or so after the press release is issued, the candidate must be available to return phone calls to radio and television stations.

Here is a rule that is important in putting out press releases: *Do not mail them — deliver them.* If you mail the press release it will not get full attention; people on the receiving end will rightfully believe that the press release has no urgency if you had dropped it in the mailbox. Have someone on the campaign staff hand deliver the press release to the media locations involved.

Weekly Newspapers

Do not overlook the weekly papers for coverage. See that they receive your press releases and that they have a file photograph of the candidate. Too many candidates treat the weekly newspapers as second-class operations. As a result they do not receive the coverage that might be available.

In some suburban and rural areas the weekly newspaper is more carefully read than the dailies because it limits its scope to news of local interest. Invite the weeklies to your press conferences. Give them the same attention that you do the dailies and it may pay off with outstanding coverage.

Buying Newspaper Space

It used to be that newspapers took advantage of political campaigns when it came to buying political advertising. Politicians paid the top price. The merchant running an ad for shoes or the movie exhibitor advertising the latest porno movie received preferential rates over politicians. Election reforms have equalized this situation in most places. It seems ironic that local newspapers would make editorial comments about the need for more citizens to seek public office, and then when candidates did file for office, the same papers would take advantage of them by charging the highest rate for political advertising.

Newspaper advertising, in the opinion of most political consultants, is not as effective as either television or radio, since more people depend on TV and radio for their news and entertainment. But I think it is important that some political ads be run in newspapers.

There are a couple of approaches you can use with newspaper ads. One of the first rules is to try to be different. Do not do what everybody else does, unless you cannot come up with anything original. If you cannot, then copy first-class ads. I think it is important that everything you do in a campaign in the way of advertising and promotion be done well. The impression that quality makes is more lasting, in my opinion, than quantity. I would rather have one really outstanding political ad in a newspaper than three bad ones.

The timing of your newspaper ads should be considered. One approach is that you can start early and run your material with some degree of regularity. The other school of thought is that most people do not pay much attention until a few days before the election and consequently any ads that you run before that time are wasted.

Let's go back to our concept that the candidate is going to emphasize three issues. You could run ads on those three issues with some regularity and get that message across.

Some people feel that you have to talk about issues in order to give people a reason to vote for you. Others feel that people do not always make up their minds based on issues. They vote for you because they know you (they may know you because of advertising) or because they like the way you look or because they feel you think the way they do. You cannot prove this theory one way or the other because people may not tell you why they vote the way they do; they may even lie to you about why they voted a certain way, especially if the real reason is one that they do not consider socially acceptable.

There are no political experts, just amateurs with varying degrees of experience. Let's assume that your election is the first Tuesday in November. You could consider starting to run some newspaper ads early in September. In October you might run two each week. During the last ten days you could consider running an ad every day and maybe even two each day.

The other theory is not to advertise until ten days or two weeks before the election and then use a saturation approach. This concept works well in a campaign going into the last two weeks that still has a large number of undecided voters. The problem is that if you wait too long with all of your media material, the undecided may no longer be undecided—they may have made the decision to vote for your opponent.

Most newspapers now require that political ads be paid for in advance. This is understandable. It is difficult to collect debts from a losing campaign that has no money and no capacity to raise any.

Another decision you need to make about your newspaper ads is whether or not to run the candidate's photograph with the material. Unless the candidate is so well-known that the name alone conjures up the face of the candidate, you should run the photograph. You also have to decide whether you will use a lot of small ads or a fewer number of large ads.

If you use an advertising agency they will take care of placing the newspaper ads for you. If you do not, the advertising department of the newspaper will help you with the format. The staff will assist you to place an ad that will please you visually in terms of composition and typesetting. They will not suggest the contents for you, so you need to know what you want the ad to say.

A final word of caution. Many newspapers restrict what you can say about an opponent in the final hours of a campaign. I know of two newspapers that will not print new charges immediately before an election, if there is not an edition before the election in which the opponent can answer those charges.

If the newspaper editorially endorses your campaign—my congratulations. If they endorsed your opponent, remember that the comics, the sports page, letters to the editor, Dear Abby, and the front page all get more attention than the editorials. In some cities, the only people who read political editorials are the editorial writers, their families, and politicians. Few readers bother to read political editorials. (In some cities you are better off having the newspaper endorse your opponent—while most editors won't admit it, many people resent having a newspaper "tell me who to vote for.") A good candidate and campaign organization can handle this situation without a great deal of difficulty. Here is one way to handle it: "This newspaper has a right to endorse anyone it wants. Its primary purpose is to report the news and as long as its editorials are confined to the editorial page, you'll hear no objection from me. The voters of this community are perfectly capable of making up their minds. They will study the issues and the candidates. How these voters react to me as a candidate is more important to me than who the newspaper selects for whatever obscure reason or special interest it may have."

If the newspaper is out to defeat you, you have a right to defend yourself and turn its endorsement of your opponent into an asset for your campaign. Candidates have been known to run against the newspaper and win. Even though a newspaper may support your opponent, it must give you equal treatment in news coverage and ad buying.

22

Political Coffees and Rallies

THE POLITICAL COFFEE SHARES SIMILARITIES with the political cocktail party, but has enough differences that it warrants a chapter of its own. The coffee as a campaign device is of rather recent vintage. It does not lend itself to a state-wide campaign because you cannot meet thousands of voters by going to coffees. It works best for geographic campaigns in which the area is not too large and there are not a tremendous amount of voters in the district.

The beauty of political coffees is that they can be held at any time of the day. You could hardly hold a political cocktail party at 9:00 A.M.

A political coffee is held in someone's home. One person on the campaign committee is in charge of arranging these coffees. Obviously, people who are friendly to your campaign host these events. They invite their friends and neighbors for the purpose of meeting the candidate. That is the basic premise — build on it from there.

I will discuss one coffee, although the candidate may attend a half dozen of these events in the same day. The number of people invited to the coffee depends on how many people the hosts can accommodate in one area of their home. I would not recommend holding a political coffee unless there is a reasonable expectation that at least twenty people will be in attendance.

You do not just invite people and then wait to see how many show up. If you want a minimum of twenty people to attend, you should invite at least forty. They can be invited by written invitation or by telephone. If you use written invitations, include an R.S.V.P. by a given date with a phone number. Do not use the "regrets only" approach because you will assume people are coming, and then be disappointed when they do not show. For some reason people do not feel a social obligation to observe good manners when it comes to political functions. Many will let you believe they will attend, and will offer no explanation when they do not show up.

One week after you have sent out the invitations, follow up with a phone call to those who have not responded. Even if you invite forty people, and all forty say they will attend, you will be lucky to have thirty when the event finally arrives.

About two days before the coffee, phone those people again who have said they are coming, and remind them again of the event, the time and the location. Don't serve anything that increases the cost to the host family. Coffee and cookies are sufficient. If you have friends who do not drink coffee, you might provide another beverage for them.

Plan the event for ninety minutes. For example, you might schedule it from 7:00 to 8:30 P.M. (which enables the candidate to attend two events in the same evening). Since few people come on time, the candidate will arrive at precisely 7:30 P.M. By that time, all of your guests will have arrived.

As your guests come in, give them name tags. This enables the candidate to call them by name during the course of his stay. Sometimes the host will introduce thirty people to a candidate and expect him to remember every name. Few people are that proficient at remembering names.

If the candidate attends a lot of coffees there is a good chance that the name of the host and hostess will not be remembered either. Therefore, the campaign person in charge of the political coffees should have the host and hostess wear name tags also, with the words "host" and "hostess" shown below the name. The purpose of any campaign device is to win votes for the candidate, and this attention to detail makes all the difference.

The first fifteen minutes of the candidate's stay is spent shaking hands, meeting, and briefly conversing with every person in attendance. A bit more attention is paid to the host and hostess.

After the first fifteen minutes the host or hostess introduces the candidate to the group. This should not be a formal introduction. A formal introduction at an informal function makes people uncomfortable; it is too slick and looks too staged (even though it is — it's staged informality). The host or hostess thanks everyone for coming and then turns the attention to the candidate. The candidate stands even though everyone else is seated. After graciously thanking the host and hostess, he may spend ten minutes with his campaign talk on "why I'm running" and "what I think is important." Then he may open the floor to questions.

There is nothing more deadly than to ask for questions and have none surface. Therefore, the campaign person in charge of organizing the coffees should have a couple of questions planted by the host and hostess. These are questions on issues that the candidate handles well. After a few questions are asked, the ice is broken and others will open up and ask a question of their own.

At 8:25 P.M. the candidate wraps it up, expresses his deep appreciation again to the host and hostess, and leaves. If there is another coffee beginning at 8:30 P.M. the candidate can arrive there at 9:00 P.M. and start the process over again.

A couple of other comments. If a member of the campaign committee can arrive at 7:00 P.M., that person can make certain that everything is handled in accordance with the plan. The brochures, bumper stickers, pins, and other material can be set out. This campaign person could leave before the coffee is over, and go to the location of the second coffee to do the appropriate advance work there too.

A nice touch that solidifies support is for the campaign person to take a photograph of the candidate with the host and hostess. This photo should be enclosed with the thank you letter that the candidate writes within seven days of the coffee.

The host and hostess should be requested to provide the campaign with the names, addresses, and phone numbers of all those in attendance. This list may then be used for many purposes, such as fund raising, recruiting workers, or as a direct mail list for a personalized letter from the candidate. (Any time we talk about a letter from the candidate, we are talking of letters prepared for his signature by the campaign committee or staff.)

The campaign coffee is an effective way of campaigning. It is time consuming, hard work, and requires an iron constitution.

Political Rallies

Nearly all political rallies are sponsored by organizations other than the candidate's own campaign committee. They may be sponsored by a political party or by organizations that traditionally are involved in political activity. Candidates attend political rallies for a variety of reasons. One of the primary reasons is that they might be conspicuous should they not attend. If you are invited to attend a rally you will almost feel obligated to attend, especially if it is one being organized by your own political party.

If all of the candidates are in attendance and all are invited to speak, you may be in for a long evening. It is best if your own remarks are brief and concise. Recognize a rally for what it is — it is usually a device to whip up the troops who already support the candidates present. You do not see rallies very often that involve opposition candidates. Those are no longer called rallies; they are called joint appearances or debates.

Often political rallies become media events. Some candidates have been known to have as many of their supporters present as possible, so that when the introduction is made, the applause is louder than it is for anyone else. Having your supporters present in great number wearing their campaign paraphernalia is a game of oneupmanship. This is one way success images are born. However, it is important that the candidate not begin taking this contrived outpouring too seriously.

One routine that can occasionally be pulled off at a rally or dinner is to stand when your candidate is introduced. Other people from your campaign who also stand then create an almost automatic effect throughout the audience. If your candidate speaks near the end or is the last speaker, he then receives a standing ovation that other candidates have not received. If your candidate is one who speaks early, then every candidate will receive a standing ovation, because no other supporters are going to stand for your candidate and not start the same kind of commotion for their own. This ploy works best when your candidate is either the last or next to last to be introduced.

Rallies are not the event they were many years ago. With the advent of television, people do not go out to political rallies looking for entertainment. However, you may occasionally be called upon to attend and participate in one of these.

23

Political Dinners

MOST POLITICAL DINNERS WILL BE hosted by a political party for its own candidates. These may be fund-raising dinners, but if so their purpose is to raise the dollars for the party itself, though a percentage may go to the candidate as a contribution from the party.

If you are the nominee of your party or if the dinner is held before your primary election, it's important that you go to the function to be seen and participate. It's true that as far as the voters are concerned, political parties are becoming less important, but they are still important to the people who attend such dinners.

I would estimate that less than five percent of the people of this nation have ever worked on a political campaign. So, that small group deserves a lot of credit (or blame — depending on how cynical the reader is) for moving the rest of the population to at least register and vote. Therefore the people at these political dinners are those who take their politics seriously. They contribute most of the money and do most of the work. They do not all do so unselfishly, but many do.

A candidate should view a political dinner of his or her own party as another organizational opportunity. Too many candidates just go to these dinners and utter a few incompetent remarks when called upon.

You should start by having crews on the street and at the parking areas around the dinner site. As people attending the dinner pull up and park, your workers ask if they can put your campaign bumper sticker on their cars.

Before people file into the dinner, make certain that one of your campaign brochures is at each dinner place. After the dinner, someone with your campaign group should pick those up left at the table. Campaign brochures are much too expensive to allow any waste.

Inside the hall, your campaign has tables set up to cover all the entrances. Your campaign volunteers ask if they can put one of your campaign buttons or stickers on each person entering. If they turn you down, just thank them politely and go on to the next person.

With this approach, your campaign and your candidate will have more campaign buttons and stickers showing than nearly any other candidate. The reason is that few candidates will go to the trouble to organize this extensively.

Another opportunity that presents itself at such dinners is picking up the names of volunteers who may wish to work on your campaign. This can be handled in one of two ways. You can have a table set up with a sign above it asking for campaign volunteers. Some people may actually go to such a table and sign up. These are the political activists, and if there is any group that will have such volunteers, it would be at such a dinner. A preferable way to recruit volunteers and other help is to enclose a card with your campaign brochure, which may contain the following information:

(Please sign and leave on table — we'll pick up)
To: Joe Candidate
          Yes I will help in the following way:
_____ I'll campaign door-to-door in my precinct.
_____ I'll contribute money.
_____ I want a yard sign.

_____ I want a bumper sticker.
_____ I'll do telephoning.
_____ I'll hold a coffee.
_____ I'm available to help in any way I can.

Signed_____

Address_____Phone_____

Experience indicates that people who want to help will fill out this card and will walk to the head table and hand it to the candidate or someone they know who is identified with the campaign.

The candidate's participation in the speaking portion of the program will depend on how the evening is planned. Occasionally, an outside speaker will be brought in, and the local candidates will merely be introduced to the crowd. Other times each candidate will be given an allotted time to speak. Do not exceed your allotted time. If you are granted ten minutes use only ten minutes. Prepare that ten-minute talk in advance. Make certain that it is well-organized and that it touches on all of the major points that you want to cover. Most candidates who are given ten minutes will "wing it," and unless they are accomplished speakers, they will not come off well. You want to come off well at *every* appearance.

Even though you may be appearing with people of your own party who are your fellow nominees, and even though none of them are running for the same office you are seeking, your goal should be to come off better than anyone else who speaks from behind that lectern. Even though you are not running against these people, you must remember that there are people in the crowd who will have to pick and choose which candidates they are going to support with their contributions. They cannot give their money to all of them. If you come off better than anyone else, some of these people may decide you are one of the bright lights of their party, and that you are someone to support now and in the future. Political careers are started at such dinners. You never know what impact any campaign appearance might have. That's why every appearance is worth doing well. In a political campaign you can never be absolutely certain what activity makes a difference; consequently whatever you do, do it well.

Political dinners can range from state-wide dinners to those of a congressional, county, city, or legislative district. You may be invited to all of these overlapping geographic dinners. They present a great opportunity to impress not only the party regulars in attendance, but also the news media invited to these functions. Your appearance and speech could make the newspapers, or radio or television newscasts.

The role you are asked to play at such a dinner will depend on the relationship of the office you are seeking to the geographic area the dinner covers. If you are running for county clerk and you are invited to a state-wide political dinner, you not only won't be asked to speak, you will not be asked to sit at the head table. The reasons are obvious. At a state-wide political dinner, there could be close to 100 party candidates for county clerk across the state; it's impossible to introduce all of them. However, if you are asked to attend a county, city, or ward dinner, you will probably be asked to sit at the head table and to make a few appropriate remarks.

Whenever you are invited to a dinner, find out from the sponsoring organization just what the ground rules are in advance. If you are going to be asked to speak, inquire about the time they want you to use and then adhere to it religiously.

24

Debates and
Joint Appearances

MANY JOINT APPEARANCES BY COMPETING candidates are labeled debates. Few of them follow a strict debate format. Most are joint appearances with a panel of news people asking questions. A typical format is as follows:

1. An opening statement by each candidate (five minutes each).

2. Alternating questions for each candidate with a brief time for the other candidate to comment on the answer (one hour).

3. A closing statement by each candidate (five minutes each).

4. A rebuttal from each candidate; the final closing (one minute each).

This kind of format is hardly a debate. Many variations exist.

One typical variation is to allow questions from the audience. Members of the audience send written questions to one panel member selected for that purpose. The question may be directed to one candidate or the other.

Often, by the time the question would be asked, the same subject has been covered by one of the members of the panel. Therefore the question may be tossed aside because there is no sense in covering the same ground.

Sometimes the audience is allowed to verbally ask questions of the candidates. This practice requires an exceedingly strong moderator, because some people will get belligerent, especially with the candidate they are not supporting. People have been known to pack these meetings for the express purpose of making their own candidate look strong and to make the opponent come off poorly. Maintaining fairness becomes difficult under such circumstances and requires a moderator or master of ceremonies who will not be easily intimidated.

Many of the concepts we covered in the chapter "Sizing Up the Competition" apply to debates or joint appearances.

When you are going to be involved in a joint appearance, stop and think about things that could make you look bad and then make certain you take care of those areas.

You can be made to look bad if:

1. *You do not appear to be informed on the issues.* It's possible you may not know everything you are asked, but you need to have a strong feel for the issues in the campaign. This is one of the reasons candidates answer different questions than they are asked — they give a short answer and then comment about something the opponent has previously said that they believe will make some points. Another ploy that can be used when asked about what you consider a nonissue or a relatively unimportant one, is to say, "On that issue, I believe my opponent and I are in basic agreement."

2. *Your opponent is able to goad you into losing your temper.* Being a political candidate requires an infinite amount of patience, as there is always someone trying to get under your skin. Learn how to keep your cool. Many candidates may be fuming on the inside but are able to appear completely in control of themselves and the situation. Voters are favorably impressed by a candidate who does not get rattled.

3. *You take too long to answer the questions.* Many candidates hurt their own chances by an inability to be brief. They will answer a question, then answer it again, and then summarize what they have already said. The candidate should not be

so brief that the necessary points are not made, but the summary of major points can be made at the end of the joint appearance.

4. *You appear to be too agreeable with the opposition.* While this may be an effective way of disarming the opponent, it may be interpreted by those watching as a sign of weakness. You should be correct, polite, but distant to the opponent. Even if it is not a debate, you can be made to look weak by appearing too conciliatory.

5. *You make arguments that overlook important factors.* Your answers may provide the opponent with an opportunity to go for your jugular. If you are going to make a point that has a counterpoint that your opponent may seize upon, bring it up before the opponent can. There is nothing more defeating than to point out the opposition's argument before he gets to it. It has the effect of minimizing his objection and it adds to your image of being a well-balanced candidate who has the ability to look at all sides of an issue.

Use the positive-negative approach to answer objections. This is an approach that many seasoned politicians use to score points in joint appearances. It's an attempt to appear positive while negating the arguments of your opponent. After the opponent has made his argument or point, you may start your statement with the following phrase or one similar to this, "That may be a valid point, however we need to consider etc., etc." People are getting tired of candidates who always appear to be negative; they don't mind candidates who are negative who go about it in a positive way. Here are some other positive-negative phrases.

"Of course people are concerned about that, but . . . "

"While that is an issue we both care about a great deal, the fact of the matter is . . . "

"No one can disagree with your concern, however your solution has some basic flaws in it which . . . "

I am sure the reader can think of other similar phrases. The advantage of these kinds of statements is that when you do say, "I couldn't disagree more," it's a solid attention-getter because you have not used it to excess during the course of the so-called debate.

Many people believe that a debate greatly influences voters. It probably does not. Unfortunately only a small percentage of the electorate in your race will see it or even know about it. They may read about it or see clips of it on the six o'clock news. The influence of the reporting media may be more important than how you believe you performed.

It's interesting that after the televised 1960 Kennedy-Nixon debates, the overwhelming majority of people felt that Kennedy had clearly won; however those who heard the debate on radio felt that Nixon had won. It is obvious, therefore, that physical appearance and the image created in a debate are more important than the arguments won or lost.

Some gamesmanship is involved in these joint appearances. Most of the arguments that go on ahead of time about the number of debates and where they will be are matters of oneupmanship.

It is advisable to talk to your opponent before the debate begins. Shake hands with him and wish him luck. He will wonder what you are up to. It may distract him.

After the joint appearance, congratulate him for an outstanding job of discussing the issues and thank him for being such a gentleman. It is more effective as a ploy if he was less than gentle during the debate. He will be unable to understand your reaction.

Occasionally you will run into a moderator who is not fair and is obviously for your opponent. You can nearly always rectify the situation with a direct approach:

> "Fairness demands that this debate be fairly moderated."
> "I think we would all agree that a debate cannot be held without an objective umpire. I would ask the moderator to apply that principle."
> "I know the moderator to be a fair person. I would hope that the moderation to this point has been an oversight and will be corrected."

None of these statements will endear you to the moderator,

but he does not support you anyway, and so you have to equalize this situation immediately.

If you can mentally prepare yourself so that you believe you belong in the office and that you deserve to win, this feeling of quiet confidence will come through in a joint appearance. Appear very relaxed before the event begins by mingling and visiting with those who are present. If your opponent tends to be on the nervous side, your apparent relaxed attitude will make his own butterflies flutter that much faster.

In summary, be prepared. Make it a game (albeit a serious one), smile, look at the audience, relax, exude quiet confidence, and you will end up on top.

25

Bumper Stickers

BUMPER STICKERS HAVE BECOME A popular method of campaign advertising. They're small moving billboards. Because of their size, the message placed on them must be limited. The candidate's name and the office being sought is the extent of the information that can be provided.

Attempts have been made to print the campaign slogan, the candidate's photo, name and the office on a bumper sticker. The problem is that everything is so small, you need to have a rear-end collision with the car bearing the sticker so you can read it.

I recommend that you print the candidate's name as large as possible and also show the office being sought somewhat smaller but still large enough to be read.

The objective of thousands of bumper stickers is to create a subliminal impact on many voters, to firmly establish the candidate's name in the minds of the voters. It can create a subconscious impact upon people — every time an individual sees that bumper sticker it makes a visual impression on his mind. Frankly, no one can prove that such approaches to campaign advertising are effective, but more significantly, no one can prove that they are not effective — therefore you should use the bumper sticker approach.

Again, stick with the campaign colors. By doing so, one method of advertising reinforces another — the bumper sticker reinforces the billboard which reinforces the yard sign which reinforces the TV ad, which reinforces the bumper sticker and so on.

Some editorial writers might like to believe that all elections are decided by people who make a careful analysis of all the issues and then select the candidate. Many people do not make up their minds until they get into the voting booth and then many of them decide based on the name that looks most familiar. I think it is safe to say that people probably don't select their candidate for president of the United States in that manner; perhaps they don't select federal office holders that way; however I believe they select from among many candidates for various offices on the basis of names that seem familiar to them.

Bumper stickers can also help create a bandwagon effect. "Boy, a lot of people are for Smith for the City Council, I must've see a hundred cars with his bumper sticker on my way home last night."

This is why everyone who is willing to put your bumper sticker on their automobile should be given two stickers — one for the front and one for the back. You get twice as many impressions that way.

Political dinners or rallies are opportunities to get many bumper stickers placed on cars. You don't pass out bumper stickers to people and hope that they will place them on their cars. The chances are very good that bumper stickers passed out at a political dinner will never be put on the cars. Instead you organize a team of your campaign volunteers to meet cars as they park for the dinner or rally and ask the drivers if you can put your bumper sticker on their cars. If and when they say yes, one person moves to the front of the car and one to the rear, and in little time two stickers are on the car. At political dinners or rallies of your own party, you'll have positive results.

This is the kind of project that should be coordinated by one person on the campaign team. A volunteer campaign worker with some imagination and leadership qualities should be put in charge of bumper stickers. That person's sole responsibility is to get all of the bumper stickers you purchase onto cars so that they can act as moving billboards. Bumper stickers do the campaign no good on a table in the campaign office.

Any event that attracts large numbers of people will draw a large number of cars, and is an event that can be worked for bumper stickers. Of course, you'll get a much higher percentage of people turning you down. If yours is a partisan race, there's a good chance that the individual you are asking at a nonpolitical function is a member of the opposition party. But even if only one in twenty agrees, look at how many cars will have your message on their bumper. That can make quite an impact upon the election if our philosophy about subliminal advertising is correct.

If you are going to attempt to put bumper stickers on cars as they park along the street or in parking lots, you must prepare those volunteers who work such a project to learn how to handle rejection. The majority of people don't want political bumper stickers on their cars. That doesn't mean they will not vote for your candidate. Many people carry their "secret" vote to the point of not advertising how they are going to vote. Therefore your volunteers must handle rejection with a great deal of courtesy.

Another way that this project can be worked is in combination with your campaign brochure. As people get out of their cars, you approach them with one of your handouts. If they say something favorable about your candidate, you then ask if you can put bumper stickers on their automobiles.

Make sure you know what your city ordinances are about such campaigning along the street.

The private parking lot is another matter. It's best to find a parking lot owner who will give you permission to work his lot as people pull in. The majority of owners will turn you down.

The chance that they will agree is greatly lessened if you just show up—clear it with the owner in advance. If the owner brings up the question of treating both candidates or parties equally, then suggest that you would hope that the same privilege would be granted to the opposition. There is a good chance they will never show up or even think of campaigning this way.

While it is a more difficult organizational problem, you can hold back your bumper stickers, and try to get thousands of them on cars in one weekend. This requires a massive effort involving many volunteers. I believe you can create a very similar effect if they all appear within a period of two or three weeks.

Another technique you can use to create this subliminal impression is to have cars with bumper stickers parked along heavily traveled streets. This creates thousands of impressions as drivers pass by. They'll remember that they have seen the candidate's name, but generally will not remember that the stickers were on parked cars as opposed to moving vehicles. The more support you can show for your candidate the better. People may be offended by big massive billboards, but hardly anyone thinks you're overdoing it with thousand of strips of paper or vinyl on auto bumpers (both front and rear, remember).

Bumper stickers are available in several forms. The cheapest are paper. They are not water resistant and the colors tend to fade when the car sits in direct sunlight for long periods of time. If you plan on using bumper stickers in the last six weeks of the campaign, then the paper stickers are probably okay. For such a short-lived exposure, you can purchase many inexpensive paper stickers.

If you want the stickers to last three months or longer, consider the more expensive vinyl stickers. They are usually water resistant and the colors will not fade as quickly as the paper strips. They also peel off of the bumper more cleanly when the campaign is over. (The paper stickers do not come off as easily and usually require a razor blade to scrape the bumper clean.) Your supporters will appreciate your thoughtfulness in using the vinyl stickers.

It's been the author's experience that bumper stickers are left on cars a lot longer after the election if the candidate wins than if he loses.

Certain colors will fade more easily than others. So-called day-glo colors will show up well, and they will visually catch the eye quicker than other colors. However, they also tend to fade rather quickly with heavy exposure to the sun. This is especially true if a day-glo color is used on a paper base. If you decide on a day-glo color, then you're more likely to be satisfied with the results if you use it on a vinyl bumper sticker.

If you're a candidate who wants and is soliciting the support of organized labor, then you want the union logo (often called the union bug) on all of your printed material. When you seek bids on these printing jobs, do not necessarily assume that the nonunion printing work will always be less expensive. Even if the union printing does cost more, you must weigh that fact against the potential support from union members. If a union member sees very little difference between the two candidates, and one uses a union print shop for his work and one does not, where do you think his vote will go? Using a union printer doesn't obligate you to organized labor's point of view on issues, but if you want the support of union members, it can make a difference. If you are an antiunion candidate, then having the union bug on your material won't make any difference anyway.

26

Yard Signs

THE YARD SIGN IS A regional campaign device. In some sections of the country it has not been used. In many communities, municipal ordinance prohibits campaign signs in the yard of a private residence. In others the size is limited by law.

If yard signs are not prohibited in your town, and if they haven't been used, you could pull a coup on all the other candidates. If you decide to use them as a surprise tactic, you don't want to get them up too soon. If you wait until about two weeks before the election, the opposition will not have time to design a sign, get them printed, secure locations, and have them placed in the yards.

Yard signs are miniature billboards. They do not permit the amount of material that can be placed on a billboard, but they do allow more latitude than bumper stickers. Stick with your campaign colors and your basic slogan. You might add the candidate's photo to the yard sign. Keep the message simple. Again, you are trying to create an impression. The vast majority of people who will see the yard sign are going to be in a vehicle passing by.

The key is to get your yard signs on streets where there is a lot of traffic. Busy intersections are top priority locations.

When you combine the impressions created from yard signs and bumper stickers you can get the candidate's name in front of many people.

One person in the campaign should be the yard sign chairman. His job is threefold: to get the signs built; to secure the locations; and to get the signs placed at the locations.

The design and printing of the yard sign is not the job of the yard sign chairman. That is tied in with the entire thrust of the campaign. It may be designed by the ad agency (if you have one) or by someone else on the campaign committee.

Getting the signs built is the first responsibility of the yard sign chairman. The yard signs must be nailed to a stake that can be driven into the ground.

Make sure the cardboard used for the signs is sturdy enough to survive the normal weather for your area. You cannot use nails only in assembling these signs, as the cardboard will immediately pull away from the stake. Drive the nail through a flat round metal piece about the size of a half dollar (used by roofers and generally available from lumberyards or hardware stores). This will secure the yard sign firmly to the stake. A large staple gun also may work.

You can use double signs which can be read no matter which direction a car is traveling on the street, or a single sheet which faces directly to the street. You have to get much closer to see a single sign, perhaps within one or two houses of the sign, than one that is double-faced, which is perceived perhaps a block away.

Securing the locations can be completed before the signs are assembled or it can be going on at the same time. Determine where you wish to place your yard signs. Drive by the locations and copy down the addresses.

Then secure a list of the registered voters. Here, we must discuss the matter in general terms, because the geographic size of your campaign will determine how long the list will be. You may need the registrations in a ward, a village, a city, or the entire county. In most jurisdictions you must pay the election commission office for this list of registered voters. Such a list will have other useful purposes during the campaign, so you will not be using it for the yard sign project alone.

In nearly all parts of the country, registered voters are listed by precinct. Get a map that outlines the precincts, usually available from the election commissioner's office, or in some jurisdictions from the city, village, or county clerk. .

Look up your desired yard sign location on the map and locate the precinct. Then go to that precinct in the list of registered voters and find the address. Presto — there's the name of the person at that address. Then refer to the phone book for the number. With this method you can put together a list of potential locations.

Another element is added if you're in a partisan race. Once you find the location and the name, you'll also learn whether the people living there are registered as Democrats, Republicans, or Independents. If they are in the same party that you are, there is a better chance that they will agree to post your sign in their yard.

Your phone approach might go like this: "Mr. Smith, I'm calling on behalf of Joyce Jones, who is a Democratic (or Republican) candidate for the city council (or whatever office). Joyce has asked me to request your permission to put one of her attractive campaign signs in your yard."

If Mr. Smith says no, the response should be something similar to this; "Well thank you anyway. I'm sorry to have disturbed you. We hope you will consider voting for Joyce Jones for the city council on November seventh."

If Mr. Smith says yes, your response goes like this: "Thank you very much Mr. Smith. Joyce will appreciate your help a great deal. We will be putting up our yard signs the first week in April. Thank you so much." Once you get an affirmative answer, wrap it up and get off the phone. As experienced salespeople say, "Don't sell past the close."

There are some important points to be made about the telephone solicitation we just presented. You don't ever tell the people you're calling that you know that they are Democrats or Republicans. By identifying yourself as a member of the party, you accomplish the desired end. A number of people (I suspect the majority) do not know that their party affiliation is a matter of public record. Most believe that their party preference is as secret as their ballot. While you may think they're stupid for not knowing any better, you are not going to get anywhere with them if they think you have invaded their privacy.

Even if they turn you down for a yard sign, remember you still want their vote. It's important to be courteous.

When they do agree to your placing a yard sign on their property, tell them approximately when it will be placed there. If you're phoning in February and you don't plan on putting up signs until April, be sure and let that fact be known, so that they don't think you've forgotten them.

Another point that may save you some expenditure of campaign money has to do with being involved in both a primary and general election. When you win the primary, give serious consideration to picking up your yard signs and storing them until the fall campaign. Those that are still in satisfactory condition can be put back up at that time. Don't pick up your yard signs without letting people know you are going to do it – they may think the sign was stolen from their yard.

A day or two after your primary victory, have campaign workers call telling them: "Mr. Smith, I'm calling on behalf of Joyce Jones to thank you for your support in the primary. With the help of people like you Joyce was able to win. You were kind enough to allow us to place one of our campaign signs in your yard. We'll pick it up within the next day or two and store it until the fall campaign. Then if we may, we'd like to put one back up again about the first week in October. Would that be okay with you?"

Most people will be agreeable to that procedure. Occasionally someone will volunteer to take the sign down on their own and store it in their garage until the fall campaign. When they do, thank them and tell them how helpful that will be. Don't under any circumstances insist on picking up the sign, because that tells supporters that you don't trust them to take the sign down and put it back up. If they are that conscientious to volunteer, there's a strong chance they'll do exactly what they said they would do. Thank them for saving someone a trip.

In October you can call and ask if the sign is back up—but better still drive by and see if it's up. If it is, you don't need to call at all. If it isn't up you can call and say: "We're planning on having all our yard signs up by the end of the week. Would you mind putting yours back up by this Saturday?"

You didn't suggest that they forgot or couldn't be trusted to remember. You told them what the yard sign game plan was and asked them to participate in that project. This approach will offend no one.

One other important point about yard signs. Campaign workers will want yard signs even if they don't live on heavily traveled streets. They are identifying with the campaign all the way. Campaign volunteers should get yard signs if they ask for one, even if they live on a dead end street. To deny a yard sign to a campaign worker, regardless of location, is shortsighted.

Once the heavily traveled streets are covered, the secondary objective should be residences close to the polling places, so that individuals who have not as yet decided about the candidates for the election get that last exposure to your candidacy before they enter the polling booth. It might make a difference—it might not—but don't overlook the chance that it will.

Yard signs can create a real bandwagon effect if you can get them up all over the city in just a few days. That takes weeks of preparation and a large crew to place them in yards. Location of yard signs is critical. A thousand yard signs buried in lightly traveled residential areas have little impact. The same number of yard signs along well-traveled streets can be an impressive campaign device. They can have a devastating impact upon the morale of your opponent's volunteers.

A byproduct of both the bumper sticker and the yard sign is the personal commitment you get from the individual who has the sticker on his car and the sign in his yard. He's going to vote for you on election day and those campaign advertisements on his property continually reinforce that decision.

27

Door-to-Door
Canvassing

DOOR-TO-DOOR CANVASSING CAN BE an effective method of campaigning but it can cost you votes if it is done incorrectly. Door-to-door canvassing is nothing more than campaigning. At one time canvassing meant actually identifying those people who were committed to you and then following through to see that those people actually got to the polls and voted. Political parties will sometimes canvass an area to identify unregistered voters, and if they appear to be of the same political persuasion to get them registered for the election and to see that they vote. In this chapter we will be referring to campaigning in neighborhoods. You can go door-to-door actually talking to people about your campaign, or you can leave campaign material at the door without ever ringing the doorbell. We'll discuss both approaches.

If campaign volunteers are going door-to-door ringing doorbells and attempting to talk to those people who answer the door, you need to make certain that the campaign has a "canned talk" that these campaigners are to use. You don't want door-to-door volunteers ad-libbing. Ad-libbing the wrong statements could cost you votes instead of gaining them.

The "canned talk" should be very brief and should be concluded by handing the individual some campaign material which has previously been discussed. The volunteer could hand them either a brochure or a handout which the resident might keep and see occasionally, and in this way be reminded to vote for your candidate.

If the resident wants to discuss issues, the campaigner should respond only to those questions on which the candidate's position is well-known to the volunteer. The volunteer should never allow himself to be drawn into an argument about issues. Complete courtesy is the rule to be followed. If the resident asks a question that the campaigner cannot answer, the response should be, "I don't know, but I'll find out and phone you with the answer." Then write down the question; and if they'll give you the phone number, jot it down so you can call them with the answer. That kind of followup could secure a vote for your candidate.

A candidate should never ask a volunteer to perform a campaign task that he or she is unwilling to do. Therefore, it's a good idea for the candidate to do some door-to-door campaigning. The candidate will get a lot more questions at the door than volunteers will. In some campaigns, it may be possible to cover nearly every house in the area involved in the election. An example might be a ward in a city election or a legislative district. A candidate who can cover nearly every house in his district can make a big difference in the results.

Another way of campaigning door-to-door can only be used by volunteers. There is more and more adverse reaction to being bothered at the door by someone campaigning for some candidate. As a result, many campaign workers are leaving material on the door without ringing the bell. The campaign brochure can be left on the doorknob so that it will be found by the resident the next time the door is opened.

One suggestion is to have an attachment stapled to your brochure which reads: "We respect your privacy too much to ring your bell to hand you our campaign brochure. We hope you'll read it and if you decide you can vote for me on election day, I'll sincerely appreciate your support."

In addition to being an approach that many people will appreciate, your own candidacy will be reinforced every time some other candidate's campaign worker rings a bell and disturbs a family's television viewing or whatever their activity may be.

If you do ring doorbells, quit by 9:30 P.M. If you disturb people as they prepare for bed, you'll lose votes. For the same reasons you should not make calls early on Saturday or Sunday mornings. People sleeping in will not appreciate being awakened by someone wanting to hand them a campaign brochure. If your people come to a home displaying your opponent's yard sign, don't waste your time going to that door and wasting a brochure.

The appearance of people doing campaigning in a neighborhood is important. If it's a working-class neighborhood, your people shouldn't canvass in a suit with shirt and tie; they ought to dress more casually. Conversely if you're working an upper-class neighborhood, wearing a business suit may be perfectly acceptable. It is difficult to develop hard and fast rules for dress and appearance because what is considered acceptable dress in Northridge, California, may be deemed a bit extreme in Bathgate, North Dakota. I merely call the matter to your attention, so that you will at least consider the possibility of a problem before you start working a neighborhood.

Up to this point we've talked about "how" you work a neighborhood, but we haven't talked about "who." It is preferable if you can have someone who lives in the neighborhood work the area. There's a chance that they'll know many people who live there and there's a better response to friends and acquaintances than to strangers. However, it's better to have a stranger work the neighborhood than not to work it at all.

Let's assume that your strategy is to work the entire community, but then you discover that you can't put together enough manpower to do it. Many candidates and their managers make the mistake of having their people work their home areas and virtually ignore the precincts where they are missing a worker. This is a mistake, in my judgment.

You need to identify the precincts where you are liable to be strong and then work those precincts in preference to the precincts where you are liable to be weak. If you're a Democrat or Republican, there are precincts in the jurisdiction that vote heavily for one or the other party. Take all the precincts in the area involved in your race and rank them from best to worst, based on either registered voters of your party or turnout of voters who traditionally vote for candidates of your party. Work the "best" areas to get out additional votes. If a precinct normally votes 70 percent for candidates of your party, then for each additional ten votes you get out, you're likely to receive seven of them and your opponent only three. That's a great ratio. You can work to make it even better.

By working with the registered voter list, you can call only on people of your party; this way you won't encourage the three-out-of-ten to vote for your opponent to get out.

Voter Registration

If you want to get additional people registered to vote for you, you have an ambitious project on your hands, but it can be done. If you consider going this route and you are in a race where you carry a party label, consult with the leader of your party to see if the party plans a voter registration drive. If they do, and they conduct it successfully, you will be the beneficiary of that effort.

If you're in a nonpartisan race and you believe that a voter registration effort can be of value to your effort, you must still identify those locations that are likely to be your strong areas. If you've come through with a primary election victory, you can determine the areas where you were strong.

Once you know which precincts you are going to canvass, you have to decide which houses you're going to contact. Are you going to call only on those houses that do not show on the voter registration list, or are you going to call on everyone?

Your approach should be similar to the following (with an

appropriate form to record the information): "Good evening, my name is Jessica Leach. I'm one of a group of volunteers who is working on a voter registration drive in this neighborhood. Would you mind if I asked you a few questions? Are you registered to vote?" If the answer is yes, you should ask if there are other people of voting age at the residence. If the answer again is yes, you then ask if they are also registered to vote. If the answer is yes, you then might continue in this manner: "In addition to working on a voter registration, I'm also working for the candidacy of Joe Smith for the city council. We'd appreciate it if you'd take the time to read our brochure and consider voting for Joe on election day. Thank you for your time and your courtesy."

You reverse the situation somewhat if you are only calling on homes that do not show registered voters. "Good evening, my name is Jessica Leach. I'm one of a group of volunteers who is working for Joe Smith for the city council. Mr. Smith has asked us not only to campaign for him, but to encourage people to get out and vote. Are you familiar with the campaign of Joe Smith for the city council?" If the answer is yes, you proceed as follows: "I wonder if you would mind if I ask you a question about that campaign? If the election were being held today, would you be *inclined* to vote for Joe Smith or his opponent, Mr. Tracy?"

At this point you're likely to get one of a variety of answers:
1. "I haven't made up my mind yet."
2. "I'm definitely for Smith."
3. "None of your business."
4. "I'm voting for Tracy. I don't like your man Smith."

If the answer is 1 or 2, "I'm glad to hear that, are you registered to vote?"

If they answer no, proceed to give them information on how to get registered. Get the person's name, address, and phone number if possible. In some states it's much easier to get voters registered than in others, so how you proceed next will be governed by the law in your state.

The reason you want the phone number is so that one of your telephone volunteers can call them before the registration deadline and see if they have in fact registered. In some areas, you can obtain the new registrations at the election commissioner's office. If they're friendly, neutral, or for you, you want to work hard to make certain that they register and vote. If they're unfriendly, neutral, or answer with 3 or 4, say, "I'm sorry to hear that. I apologize for disturbing you this evening. Good night!"

Don't go out and register voters who are going to vote for your opponent! This is why you want to qualify the prospect, as successful salespeople know. If he's for your opponent, let your opponent identify him and get him registered.

Going out and identifying unregistered voters is a laborious and expensive process in time, manpower, and money. You have limited resources (most campaigns do anyway) so you have to make the judgment as to whether this is the way you want to use those resources.

28

Use of the Telephone

THE USE OF THE TELEPHONE as a campaign device is diminishing in popularity in many parts of the country. Many people have requested unlisted numbers to avoid getting telephone solicitations at home. This is perfectly understandable. People have telephones installed for their own convenience, not for the use of telephone hucksters.

I'm afraid my prejudice against the use of the telephone as a campaigning tool is showing. However, I'll try to be as objective as I can, because I know of some candidates who believe the use of the phone made a difference in a close campaign.

The most common use of the phone is to call people and ask them to vote for your candidate. The message might be similar to the kind of information you'd provide if you were calling at their front door. However, you can't hand them a brochure over the telephone, so the message has to be more thorough.

Never argue with anyone over the phone about your candidate or some of the positions he has taken. When you call someone who is irritated, terminate the conversation as courteously and quickly as possible.

It is possible to test the person's reaction before you identify your candidate. That way if the person being called gets very irritated, he cannot get miffed at your candidate because you haven't yet identified your candidate. You may start with a message similar to the following: "Hello, I'm Darlene, I'm calling about the city election for City Council that is coming up next Tuesday. Do you plan on voting next Tuesday?"

If the person is going to snap your head off, he will do it at this point. If he gets irritated or worse, terminate the call immediately: "I'm sorry to have troubled you. Have a nice evening."

If he does not get irritated but appears to be receptive to your call or at least neutral, you can go on. "We're glad to hear that you will vote next Tuesday. This is an important election, Mr. Springfield. We're asking for your vote for Joe Smith for City Council. We need your vote. Will you seriously consider voting for Joe?"

This is a better approach than asking directly if they will vote for Joe. People still believe in the sanctity of the secret ballot and many will resent any question that directly asks how they will vote. They may respond positively to a question about how they would be inclined to vote if the election were held today, because it doesn't cross that invisible line that separates a secret ballot from your inquiry.

If they say they'll consider voting for your candidate, there's a better than average chance that they've already made up their minds in your favor.

Keep a record of every phone call that is made. On a card record the name, address, and phone number. The card will look like this:

Name_____ Phone_____
Address_____

For us _____
Against us _____
Neutral _____
Irritated – call terminated _____
____ possible contribution   ____call on election day
____ possible worker   ____other – make note
____ wants a yard sign   _____

Of course, if you're calling late in the campaign, there may not be much opportunity to follow up with the card, unless this is a person whom you think should be called on election day to make sure that he or she votes. Cards like this can also be used early in the campaign when you're lining up workers and an organization.

When you get a favorable response on a phone call, and the person indicates he'd like to do something to help, you could suggest a yard sign, if you still have some to put up, or you might suggest: "As you know it takes money to run political campaigns and while people like myself volunteer our services, printing, phones, and all forms of advertising are terribly expensive. So Joe would be most appreciative if you would like to make a campaign contribution."

If the reaction is quite positive, you could ask if he would like you to send someone out to pick up the contribution or if he'd like to mail it in. Of course, if he wants to mail it, be sure he has the correct address. You won't get many people volunteering to give away money.

Another device you may want to consider is a recorded message from the candidate. These can be completely automated so that the entire system is done by computer. However, it is too costly and too sophisticated for most campaign treasuries. In addition the practice appears to be in danger of being outlawed as an invasion of privacy.

The individually placed call by a volunteer who delivers a message, as we suggested earlier, to identify the prospect as at least a neutral, can then be followed by a recorded phone message from the candidate. You would need some technical advice about how to establish this with your phones, but it can be as simple as a cassette recording. If you consider this idea, obtain some advice from a sound technician on how to handle it.

Never allow your telephone volunteers to make up their own messages. The communication must be decided in advance. Otherwise you'll have many messages going out to voters that will be as different as the volunteers participating.

If you can bring volunteers together at a campaign head-quarters to use a bank of telephones, you receive mutual reinforcement. They are in the effort together and the peer pressure has a positive impact. If the volunteer is to make the phone calls from his or her home, it's tough to get started. It's easier to sit down and watch television.

Don't give a volunteer a list of two hundred people to call. It's difficult for a campaign worker, no matter how dedicated, to start on such a list. Too often it's put off indefinitely; in some cases the cards are filled out with phony information just to take the pressure off.

If volunteers are going to make their phone calls from home, never issue them a list longer than twenty calls. People can visualize themselves making twenty calls, but not 200. If the calls are to be made over a period of time, you may ask the volunteer to make an additional twenty calls next week, but only after the first assignment is completed.

This is a solid campaign rule to follow for all activities. Always make assignments in small bites that people can accept and handle. If you use this incremental approach, there's a better chance the work will be accomplished. If the job looks insurmountable it may never be started.

One device that you may consider acknowledges the fact that people resent having their privacy invaded with campaign phone calls. The idea is to place a statement in your other advertising material indicating that you will not be using the telephone as a campaign device: "Joe Smith, candidate for city council, respects your privacy. Because of this respect, neither Joe Smith nor his campaign workers will disturb you by making campaign telephone calls to your home."

Don't go this route unless you are absolutely committed to it. If you think you'd change your mind later in the campaign, then don't do it. This approach does have some positive sides. If we are correct, that people do resent being interrupted by a telephone message, then every time they see that statement in a political brochure or in a newspaper ad, their reaction to your candidacy will be positive, or at worst, neutral. In addition, if they've seen your message, you receive reinforcement every time some other campaign calls. You have to weigh these advantages against whatever support you believe a telephone campaign will generate.

When you solicit people to work on a telephone campaign, attempt to get those who do not object to talking to strangers on the phone. Do not minimize the difficulty of the task you are asking them to perform. People involved in political campaigns either as candidates or in leadership positions have a tendency to regard themselves as super salespeople. As a result they often tend to sell people on accepting tasks in a campaign that those people will not perform well. You are much better off not selling people on difficult tasks. Of course, don't overreact and make the job sound worse than it is. Describe the function factually, so that when people agree to do it, they know exactly what they are getting into.

29

The Day
of the Election

ELECTION DAY IS THE DAY you've all been working toward. All of the work of many months, and perhaps the planning of several years, come to fruition on this day.

In this chapter I will discuss what can be done on election day. Many close campaigns are decided because one candidate and his campaign team worked right up until the time the polls closed and the other candidate sat back and waited for the results.

While it may be unfortunate, it is a fact that many people do not make up their minds about *some* races until they are actually in that election booth and are ready to make the selection. When this kind of situation prevails, it is obvious that, at least as far as that campaign is concerned, our undecided voter doesn't feel very strongly about the issues. In fact, there's a great likelihood that he doesn't know what those issues are.

It has been my feeling for a number of years that if a voter is still undecided when he gets into that booth, he would be better off skipping that race. To vote for one of the candidates because you like the ring of his name is not casting a well-informed vote. If a voter picks the one who is of the same political party that he belongs to, there is at least some reason for his choices, which is better than no reason at all.

Notwithstanding my feelings, the fact remains that far too many people decide how they are going to vote in some races based on reasoning that does not make much sense. If you are in a close race, you have to go after this nonissue, uninformed vote. The trouble with a close race is that you may not know it is close until you've lost it by a few hundred or a few thousand votes.

People may make up their minds in the voting booth based on one of the following nonsensical reasons:

1. *They like the looks of the candidate.* You cannot help what the candidate looks like, but if the candidate conducts himself with the image of success (discussed in an earlier chapter), it can make a difference to this kind of voter. There's not much you can do about this on election day, except to keep your campaign ads going that day.

2. *The candidate must be popular because they have seen a lot of bumper stickers and yard signs.* People may decide on who to vote for based on which candidate they think is the most popular. For this reason you want yard signs in the entire area around the polling places, while of course observing the legal requirements on the distance signs must be from the polling place. This is another reason why you want a lot of bumper stickers throughout the community.

3. *They vote for the candidate who was the last to ask for their vote.* For this reason, you may want to have campaign workers as close to the polling place as the law allows. The volunteers hand people your campaign card and actually ask them to vote for your candidate. "Will you please consider voting for John Smith for the city council?" They shouldn't hand out an elaborate brochure, because there obviously isn't going to be time for voters to read it. A simple campaign card with the candidate's name, the office being sought, and your campaign slogan is all that is necessary.

If you used telephone canvassing to identify your supporters, you will have made a card record on these people. You can increase your vote by making certain that these people vote on election day with a telephone followup. Your workers can call the people who indicated they were going to vote for you and follow through to make certain that they do get out and vote. Since the polls open early in the morning, don't start this followup practice until noon. This gives voters up to five hours to have voted before they're called. When you call at noon, identify yourself as a member of the Smith campaign committee. "Mr. Longman, this is Mrs. Headrick with the Smith for Council Committee. Your support is very important to Mr. Smith. Have you voted yet, Mr. Longman?"

If Mr. Longman indicates he's already voted, you are finished. Thank him and hang up (and hope he voted for your candidate). If Mr. Longman tells you he has not voted yet, continue along these lines: "Do you plan on voting today?"

If he says yes, ask him approximately what time he plans on voting. Asking the question about the time gives him a self-designated goal for voting, and in most cases people will try to meet that commitment.

If he says he's going to vote at 5:00 P.M. you then have another decision to make. You can call him back at 6:00 or 6:30 P.M. to see if he has voted, or you can take his word for it that he would vote.

If you're going to work every vote possible, you'll call him again and ask him if he's voted. The call can be apologetic in nature if necessary. If he says he still hasn't voted, you can again make your plea that his vote is vitally needed in this election.

The safest way is to follow up every vote until about an hour before the polls close. There's no sense in calling people if no time is left to get from their homes to the polls.

I haven't mentioned offering rides to the polls, because the laws vary among the states and other political subdivisions. If it is permissible to drive people to polls so that they can vote, this is another possibility to get votes for your candidate.

Giving people rides to the polls is strictly an election day activity, but it must be planned weeks ahead of the day itself. You want to get only your supporters to the polls—you don't want to take people to the polls who are going to vote for your opponent. Therefore under no circumstances would you run an ad in the newspaper listing a phone number that people may call if they need a ride. Let your opponent get his own voters to the polls.

Qualify your voters before you take them to the polls. You recall in the chapter on the use of the telephone, we discussed making a card record of the people who support the candidate. Those are the people you are willing to take to the polls, if the law in your political subdivision permits such activity.

There are other activities that can be used on election day. You can use the human billboard approach. Determine the heavily traveled traffic routes in your area, and then have campaign workers, about a block apart, holding your campaign signs. You might stretch these campaign workers out for miles depending on how many are available. This kind of dedication by campaign workers can be impressive to voters who haven't yet made up their minds. There's not a great deal of sense in doing this in the morning as people are going to work—some of them will have already voted and the sign isn't going to change that vote. Those who haven't as yet voted will see your human billboards on their way home. There's more to be gained using this technique the night before election day and election day evening than on election day morning.

Some candidates stop all of their media advertising on the evening before the election. This makes sense as far as television is concerned. TV ads shown election night are too late to do much good. It is money thrown away. However morning newspaper ads should be run. Those ads are seen before people vote and they are just as valid as newspaper ads appearing the night before. They may be even better, because the message is seen even closer to the time they will be voting. For the same reason, continue your radio advertising on election day until about 6:00 P.M.

One approach you can use involves television on election day. Notify the TV news departments where and what time the candidate is going to vote. Make this early in the morning. There's a chance that the voting candidate will be shown on the twelve o'clock news. This additional exposure could pick up a few votes. Whether or not the TV news cameras will show up to film your candidate going into the voting booth may depend on the office you are seeking and how newsworthy the media considers that office. But it doesn't hurt to notify them — they may show up.

Occasionally, on the night before the election, or on election day itself, the media will ask the candidate for any comments now that the campaign has been concluded. There is often a temptation to get in that one last shot at the opponent. Some candidates really zero in and hit hard. Consider this carefully. People often get sick and tired of political campaigns. That last shot may cost you votes. It is doubtful that it will win you many. Your best chance with such a "final" statement is to take the statesman approach.

"I realize that people get weary of campaigns and the same is true of candidates. I'm sure both of us are glad to see it end. I want to compliment my opponent for running an aggressive, hard-hitting campaign. I hope that we have performed satisfactorily in defining the issues for the voters. It's now all in the hands of the voters. We will abide by their decision. This participation, not only by the candidates, but by all of the volunteers and the voter, is what is important. The American political system is alive and well and I'm just grateful for the privilege of participating both as a candidate and a voter."

This kind of statement is more likely to gain votes than lose them for your campaign. The public can identify with it. They probably are weary of all of the political ads and shows on television, and you're agreeing with them.

By calling your opponent aggressive and hard-hitting, you seem to be paying him a compliment. However, many people don't care for that description; it may lose him some votes.

The tenor of the talk is one of a proper amount of humility. If people who haven't made up their minds see you on television making such a gracious statement, you have a great chance of winning their votes, especially if in the same news sequence your opponent goes for your jugular. The contrast will gain votes for you.

30

The Victory Party

THE SIZE OF THE ELECTION night victory party will depend on the kind of office you're seeking and the number of volunteers working on your campaign. If you're running for governor, you'll have a different kind of problem than if you're seeking a seat on the local school board. Many campaigns or the candidates themselves incur unnecessarily large expenses because they don't know how to properly plan an election night party.

Let's begin with the small party that could be held at your own home. This kind of party is fairly easy to control as far as participants are concerned; hopefully only those people invited will attend.

One cardinal rule applies to election night parties. Never make such an event a fund raiser—those volunteers who worked for you will feel that you're squeezing every last bit of blood from them. Charging an admission price to your workers to come to a party where they will sweat out the results of their own efforts will only alienate them, and they may never lift a finger for you again. The candidate is much better off paying for such a party completely out of his own pocket than turning off those people who work for him.

In most political subdivisions, the cost of an election night party is a legitimate campaign expense, so calculate enough money in your budget to cover it. It is easiest to control costs at a party if it is held in your own home. But this, of course, restricts the number of people you can invite. At a party in your home, people will not usually get upset if you run out of refreshments; they would if the refreshments were cut off at a commercial establishment.

If you plan to have a party in your home, make certain that you invite everyone who played a major role in your campaign. This includes every person who held any kind of title, even if it was precinct captain. If you must err on the invitation side, you're better off inviting more than you think deserve to be invited than fewer.

Make certain a sufficient number of television sets and radios are available. If people are going to be in the living room, dining room, family room, den, recreation room, or kitchen, put a television set in each of these rooms. This helps distribute the crowd among the rooms and avoids everyone clustering around one television set. People who work on political campaigns usually have an interest in all of the races.

If you need to have your campaign party in a commercial establishment, crowd control is much more difficult and there are no absolutely correct answers. No matter how careful you are, you're going to have some problems.

One of the biggest problems is the "political freeloader." These are the people who always have an excuse when they are called and asked to perform some campaign task; yet, on election night, these people have an uncanny antenna for ferreting out the campaign parties where free drinks might be had.

The location of an election party is difficult to keep secret. You need to tell the news media, who may want to come and get a statement from the victorious candidate. Since you will be inviting all of your campaign workers, it will not be difficult for anyone who is interested to find the location.

There are several ways that you can control the cost of a large campaign party. Determine which one or combination fits your needs.

1. Allow admission by ticket only. Everyone who is invited receives an advance ticket and there is no other admission. The campaign chairman should have an extra supply of tickets in case a known campaign worker shows up at the door without a ticket. Tickets can be sent to news media people, so that they do not have trouble getting in. Don't forget to see that tickets go to members of the candidate's family. By controlling the number who get in, you can control the bar cost. Nearly every professional establishment can tell you how many drinks are likely to be consumed based on the size of the crowd you expect. Another advantage of the ticket approach is that you keep out the freeloader. This will delight the actual workers on the campaign who have no use for the political freeloader.

2. Allow anyone to be admitted, but shut off the bar at a given time, thereby cutting down the potential for tremendous cost overruns.

3. Use a cash bar approach, but provide free drink passes to your campaign workers. For example, you might give three free drink passes to every invited volunteer, and with the management to pay for the drinks from every card turned in. You certainly can control this cost, because you control the number of tickets printed. It's a good idea for the campaign chairman to have a few extra tickets in his pocket to take care of those situations where a foul-up occurs.

4. Limit the bar facilities. This controls the cost but it may also make your own people unhappy. However, you can control the cost if it's difficult for people to get to the bar for a drink.

5. Provide a certain amount of liquor, but shut the bar off or revert to a cash bar after that is gone.

6. In some facilities, you can rent the space and operate your own bar. Legal requirements vary in jurisdictions and most forbid the gift of liquor from a dealer. It may be worth checking out.

Another important matter to consider on election night is a facility for the candidate to accept and make telephone calls.

Hopefully in your campaign one of the calls will be a congratulatory message from your defeated opponent.

The news media not present may want to telephone you for an interview. Often times radio and television reporters will ask if they can record a statement over the telephone to play on a news broadcast. So it is important that the candidate have a statement in mind when victory comes. (I don't believe in preparing concession speeches in advance—don't plan on losing.)

Have a private room where the candidate can take these telephone messages. They cannot be handled amid a throng of people. If television and radio people are likely to come and interview, the victorious candidate should have a room where this can be done, and where the questions and answers can be heard without shouting.

It is absolutely essential that the victorious candidate doesn't celebrate too much—he must keep a clear head. If he must celebrate, he should do it later with his closest campaign associates and friends.

Establish a time for the election night party to end. The only time this creates a severe problem is when the race is so close that the results are not known by the time you close down the party. I realize that many campaign groups will not want to disperse until the results are known, but if it is so close that you have to wait for the absentee and disabled ballots you may not know for several days anyway. You have to decide how long you are going to hang in there. In my opinion it is better to end the full-blown election night party and let the candidate and his closest campaign workers and advisors adjourn to a private home to await the final results. In this day of computer counted ballots, the long delay is not as common as it once was.

My closing advice to candidates on election night is three-fold: be extra appreciative of the volunteers who helped you, win or lose; be gracious in defeat should that happen; and be magnanimous in victory.

Conclusion

THIS BOOK HAS BEEN FILLED with information about how to organize and win a political campaign. Everything will not go according to the book in your campaign. Problems will come up; the best laid plans will go astray. Flexibility in a candidate and the key campaign people is essential.

Some advice for candidates—don't take yourself too seriously. An ad agency or your campaign people may put together outstanding media material. Don't start considering yourself a celebrity. Don't start believing you are something special, set head and shoulders above the electorate and your workers. In a democracy, you are not special. You have asked to be a servant of the people—remember that a servant is not the master. The electorate is the ultimate master in a democracy. Don't become too impressed with the trappings of the office, or you'll get out of touch with those you're purported to serve.

I have seen people virtually change overnight when they made the transition from candidate to office holder. They no longer wanted to be called by their first name, but they expected to be called Commissioner, Councilwoman, Congressman, or whatever. As a result they were indicating they were

not yet ready for the office and in far too many cases their performance as an office holder proved it.

A political candidate can have great confidence in his or her
own ability and own political judgments, and still maintain a
sincere humility that provides the necessary balance to make
him or her a good public servant.

Too many candidates and office holders have a condescend-
ing attitude toward the voter. They consider the electorate a
group to be manipulated for their own purposes. You can run
an intelligent, well-organized, and soundly administered campaign, maintain the proper respect for yourself, and more important, for the people you ask to serve—the voters.

Index